R 1294 EL1/9

WILLOBIE HIS AVISA

1594

AN ESSAY ON *WILLOBIE HIS AVISA*

ELIZABETHAN AND JACOBEAN QUARTOS

ELIZABETHAN AND JACOBEAN QUARTOS
EDITED BY G. B. HARRISON

WILLOBIE HIS AVISA

1594

With an Essay on
Willobie His Avisa
BY G. B. HARRISON, M.A.

EDINBURGH
at the University Press

This edition published in 1966
in the United States of America
by Barnes & Noble, Inc.,
and in Great Britain
by Edinburgh University Press,
is reproduced from the series
BODLEY HEAD QUARTOS
published by
John Lane The Bodley Head Ltd., London
between 1922 and 1926

Printed in the United States of America

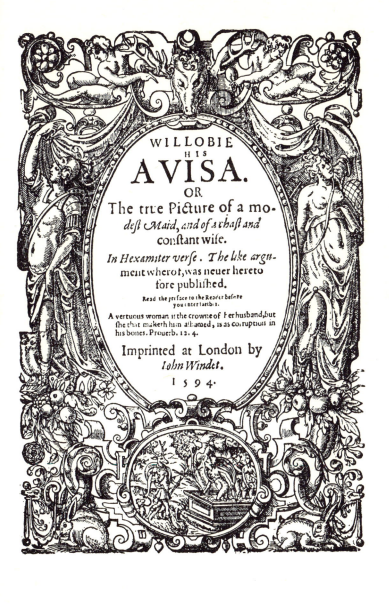

WILLOBIE
HIS
AVISA.
OR.
The true Picture of a mo-
dest Maid, and of a chast and
constant wife.

In Hexamiter verse . The like argu-
ment wherof, was neuer hereto
fore published.

Read the preface to the Reader before
you enter farther.

A vertuous woman is the crowne of her husband, but
she that maketh him ashamed, is as corruption in
his bones. Prouerb. 12. 4.

Imprinted at London by
Iohn Windet.

1 5 9 4.

To all the constant Ladies & Gen-
tlewomen of England that feare God.

Ardon me (sweete Ladies,) if at this present, I depriue you of a iust Apology in defence of your constant Chastities, deserued of many of you, and long sithence promised by my selfe, to some of you: and pardon mee the sooner, for that I haue long expected that the same should haue beene perfourmed by some of your selues, which I know are well able, if you were but so wellwilling to write in your owne praise, as many men in these dayes (whose tounges are tipt with poyson) are too ready and ouer willing, to speake and write to your disgrace. This oc-casion had bene most fit, (publishing now the praise of a constant wife) if I had bene but almost ready. But the future time may agayne reueale as fit a meanes heereafter for the perfourmance of the same: if so it seeme good to him that moderateth all. Concerning this booke which I haue presumed

to dedicate to the safe protection of your accustomed courtesies; if yee aske me for the persons: I am altogether ignorant of them, and haue set them downe onely as I finde them named or disciphered in my author. For the trueth of / [*2 his action, if you enquire, I will more fully deliuer my opinion hereafter. Touching the substance of the matter it selfe, I thinke verily that the nature, woordes, gestures, promises, and very quintessence, as it were, is there liuely described, of such lewd chapmen as vse to entise silly maides, and assayle the Chastity of honest women. And no doubt but some of you, that haue beene tried in the like case, (if euer you were tryed,) shall in some one part or other acknowledge it to bee true. If mine Author haue found a Brytaine Lucretia, or an English Susanna, enuy not at her prayse (good Ladies) but rather endeuor to deserue the like. There may be as much done for any of you, as he hath done for his A vi s a. Whatsoeuer is in me, I haue vowed it wholy, to the exalting of the glory of your sweete sex, as time, occasion and ability shall permit. In the meane time I rest yours in all dutyfull affection, and commend you all to his protection, vnder whose mercy we enioy all.

Your most affectionate,
Hadrian Dorrell. /   [*2ᵛ

To the gentle & courteous Reader.

I is not long sithence (gentle Reader) that my very good frend and chamber fellow M. Henry Willobie, a yong man, and a scholler of very good hope, being desirous to see the fashions of other countries for a time, departed voluntarily to her Maiesties seruice. Who at his departure, chose me amongst the rest of his frendes, vnto whome he reposed so much trust, that he deliuered me the key of his study, and the vse of all his bookes till his returne. Amongest which (perusing them at leysure,) I found many prety & witty conceites, as I suppose of his owne dooing. One among the rest I fancied so much, that I haue ventered so farre vpon his frendship, as to publish it without his consent. As I thinke it not necessary, to be ouer curious in an other mans labour, so yet something I must say for the better vnderstanding of the whole matter. And therefore, first for the thing it selfe, whether it be altogether fayned, or in some part true, or altogether true; and yet in most part Poetically

shadowed, you must giue me leaue to speake by con-
iecture, and not by knowledge. My coniecture is doubt-
full, and therfore I make you the Iudges. Concerning
the name of A vi s a, *I thinke it to be a fained name,*
like vnto Ouids Corinna; *and there are two causes*
that make mee thus to thinke. First, for that I neuer
heard of any of that name that I remember, and next
for that | in a voide paper rolled vp in this boke, I [*3
found this very name A v i s a, *written in great letters*
a prety distance asunder, & vnder euery letter a word
beginning with the same letter, in this forme.

A. V. I. S. A.
Amans.   vxor.   inuiolata. semper.   amanda.

That is in effect. A louing wife, that neuer vio-
lated her faith, is alwaies to be beloued. *Which*
makes me coniecture that he minding for his recreation
to set out the Idea of a constant wife, (rather describing
what good wiues should doe then registring what any
hath done) deuised a womans name, that might fitly
expresse this womans nature whom he would aime at:
desirous in this (as I coniecture) to imitate a far off,
ether Plato *in his Common wealth, or* More *in his*
Vtopia. This my surmise of his meaning, is confirmed
also by the sight of other odd papers that I found,
wherein he had, as I take it, out of Cornelius Agrippa,
drawen the seuerall dispositions of the Italian, the

Spanyard, the French man, the German, and the English man, and how they are affected in loue. The Italian dissembling his loue, assaileth the woman beloued, with certaine prepared wantonnesse: he praiseth her in written verses, and extolleth her to the Heauens.

The Spanyard is vnpatient in burning loue, very mad with troubled lasciuiousness, hee runneth furiously, and with pittyfull complaintes, bewailing his feruent desire, doth call vpon his Lady, and worshippeth her, but hauing obtained his purpose maketh her common to all men.

The Frenchman endeuoreth to serue, he seeketh to pleasure his woman with songes, and disports &c.

The Germane & Englishman being nigher of nature, are inflamed by little and little, but being enamored, they instantly require with arte, and entice with giftes &c. Which seue/rall qualities are [*3ᵛ *generally expressed by this Author in the two first trials or assaultes made by the noble man, and the lustie Caualieros, Captaines, or Cutters &c. Signifying by this generalitie that our noble men, gentlemen, captaines, and lusty youthes haue of late learned the fashions of all these countries, how to sollicit their cause, & court, their Ladies, & louers, & this continueth from the second Canto, to the ende of the two and twentieth.*

After this he comes to describe these natures againe in particular examples more plainely, and beginneth first with the French man vnder the shadow of these Letters D. B. *from the three and twentieth Canto vnto the end of the three and thirtieth. Secondly the Englishman or Germane, vnder these Letters* D. H. *from the* 34. *Canto vnto the ende of the forty three. Lastly the Spanyard and Italian, who more furiously inuadeth his loue, & more pathetically indureth then all the rest, from the forty foure Canto to the ende of the booke. It seemes that in this last example the author names himselfe, and so describeth his owne loue, I know not, and I will not bee curious.*

All these are so rightly described according to their nature, that it may seeme the Author rather meant to shew what suites might be made, and how they may be answeared, then that there hath bene any such thing indeede.

These thinges of the one side leade me to thincke it altogether a fained matter, both for the names and the substance, and a plaine morrall plot, secretly to insinuate, how honest maides & women in such temptations should stand vpon their guard, considering the glory & praise that commendes a spotlesse life, and the blacke ignominy, & foule contempt that waiteth vpon a wicked and dissolute behauiour.

Yet of the other side, when I do more deepely con-

sider of it, | *& more narrowly weigh euery par-* [*4
*ticular part, I am driuen to thinke that there is some
thing of trueth hidden vnder this shadow. The reasons
that moue me are these, First in the same paper where
I found the name of* A V I S A *written in greate
letters, as I said before, I found this also written with
the Authors owne hand, videlicet,* Yet I would not
haue *Auisa* to be thought a politike fiction, nor a
truethlesse inuention, for it may be, that I haue
at least heard of one in the west of England, in
whome the substaunce of all this hath bene
verified, and in many thinges the very wordes
specified: which hath indured these and many
more, and many greater assaultes, yet, as I heare,
she standes vnspotted, and vnconquered.

*Againe, if we marke the exact descriptions of her
birth, her countrie, the place of her abode, and such
other circumstances, but especially the matter and
manner of their talkes and conferences, me thinkes it a
matter almost impossible that any man could inuent
all this without some ground or foundation to build on.*

*This inforceth me to coniecture, that though the
matter be handled poetically, yet there is some thing
vnder these fained names and showes that hath bene
done truely. Now iudge you, for I can giue no sentence
in that I know not. If there bee any such constant wife,
(as I doubt not but there may bee) I wish that there*

*were more would spring from her ashes, and that all
were such. VVhether my Author knew, or heard of any
such I cannot tell, but of mine owne knowledge I dare
to sweare, that I know one.* A. D. *that either hath, or
would, if occasion were so offered, indure these, and
many greater temptations with a constant mind, and
setled heart. And therfore here I must worthely
reprehend the enuious rage, both of Heathen Poets,
and of some Christian and English writers, which* | [*4ᵛ
*so farre debase the credite and strength of the whole
sexe, that they feare not with lying toungs wickedly to
publish, that there are none at all that can continue
constant, if they bee tried. Hereof sprang these false
accusing speeches of the old Poets.*

Ludunt formosæ, casta est, quam nemo rogauit.

> *Faire wenches loue to play.*

And they are onely chast, whome no man doth assay.

> *And againe*

Rara auis in terris, nigroq; simillima cygno,
Fœmina casta volat.

*A rare-seene bird that neuer flies, on earth ne yet in
 aire,*

*Like blackish Swan, a woman chast; if she be yong
 and faire.*

 *This false opinion bred those foule-mouthed speeches
of Frier* Mantuan, *that vpbraides all women with
fleeting vnconstancy. This made* Ariosto *and others*

to inuent, and publish so many lewd and vntrue tales
of womens vnfaithfulnes. And this is the cause, that
in this booke ye shall so often find it obiected against
A V I S A by all her sutors, that no woman of what
degree so euer can be constant if she be much requested,
but that the best will yeeld. But the best is, this common
and course conceit is receiued but onely among common,
lewd, & carelesse men, who being wicked themselues,
giue sentence of all others, according to the loose and
lawlesse humors wherewithall they feele their owne
straying and wandring affections to be infected. For
they forsooth, because in diuers and sundrie places, (as
they often wickedly boast) they may for an Angell and a
great deale lesse haue hired nagges to ride at their
pleasure, such as make a sinnefull gaine of a filthy
carkasse; because in other countries, where stewes and
brothelhouses are winckt at, they see oftentimes, the
fairest and not the meanest flocke to the fellowship of
such filthy freedome, Thinke presently, that it is but a
mony matter, or a little intreatie, to ouer/throw [A 1
the chastity of any woman whatsoeuer. But if all
women were in deede such as the woman figured vnder
the name of A V I S A either is, or at least is supposed
to bee, they should quickly restore againe their auncient
credite and glory which a few wicked wantons haue
thus generally obscured. In the twentie and seuen
Canto, I find how D. B. perswadeth with A. that it is

little sinne or no fault to loue a frend besides her husband. VVhereupon, inquiring more of the matter I haue heard some of the occupation verifie it for a trueth: That among the best sort, they are accompted very honest women in some cities now, that loue but one frend besides their husband, and that it is thought amongst them a thing almost lawfull. If this be true, (as I hardly thincke it to bee true, because wicked men feare not to report any vntrueths) but if it be true, I feare least the ripenesse of our sinne cry to the Lord for vengeance against vs, that tremble not at the remembrance of Gods iudgements, that hath bound a heauy curse & woe vpon the backe and conscience of them, That speake good of euill, and euill of good. *that is, such as are growne to that pointe, that they are no longer ashamed of their sinne, nor care for any honesty, but are become wilfully desperate in the performance of all kind of impiety.*

But I leaue this to the godly preachers to dilate more amply. And to returne to my purpose, although I must confesse that of all sortes of people, there haue bene & will be still some loosely and lewdly giuen, yet this can bee no excuse to lauishe tounges, to condemne all generally. For, I dare to venter my hand, and my head vpon this point, that, let the foure moral vertues be in order set downe.

Prudence
Fortitude
Temperance
Iustice

and let the holy scrip-

tures be searched from the beginning to the end, & | [A 1 ᵛ
*let all the ancient histories both ecclesiasticall and pro-
phane be thorowly examined, and there will bee found
women inough, that in the performance of all these
vertues, haue matched, if not ouermatched men of euery
age, which I dare my selfe, to verifie in their behalfes
vpon the venter and losing of my credite, if I had time
and leasure. Among infinite numbers to giue you a taste
of one or two: for wisedome, and Iustice, what say you
to* Placilla, *wife to the Emperour* Theodosius? *She
was wont euery day in her owne person, to visite the
sicke, the poore, and the maymed*: *And if at any time
shee saw the Emperour declining from Iustice to any
hard course, she would bid him* Remember himselfe,
from whence he came, & what he was, in what state
hee had bene, and in what state he was now; which
if he would do, he should neuer wax proud nor
cruell, but rather humble, mercyfull and iust.

Theodor-
et.
eccles.
hist. lib.
5. cap. 17.

For temperance, how say you to the wife of one
Pelagius, *of* Laodicea, *which being yong her selfe,
and married to a yong and lusty man, was yet notwithstanding contented willingly, to forbeare carnall
pleasure, during her whole life. I bring not this
womans example, for any liking I haue to her fact,
being lawfully married, but rather, against the
curious carpers at womens strength, to proue that some
women haue done that, which few men can doe.*

Theodor.
eccl. hist.
li. 4 c. 10.

Eusebius
libr. 8.
cap. 24.

For Fortitude and temperance both, I finde, that in Antioche, *there was a noble woman with her two daughters, rather then they would be defloured, cast themselues all willingly into a great riuer, and so drowned themselues.*

cap. 27.
Loke for
Blandina
in Euse-
bius, a
rare ex-
ample of
constancy
&
fortitude.

And also, that in Rome *there was a Senatours wife, who when she heard, that there were messengers sent from* Maxentius *the tirant, to bring her vnto him, perforce to be rauished of him; and seing that her husband was not of ability | and power to defend* [A2 *her, she vsed this pollicy. Shee requested that they wold giue her leaue to put on som better apparel & to attire her selfe more decently: which being graunted, and she gotten into a chamber by her selfe, she tooke a sword and perced her selfe to the hart, rather then she would be counted the Emperours whore.*

By this may be seene what might be sayd in this argument, but leauing this to some other time, or to some other better able; I returne to my author.

For the persons & matter, you haue heard my con-iecture, now for the manner of the composition, dispo-sition, inuention, and order of the verse, I must leaue euery mans sence to himselfe, for that which pleaseth me, may not fancy others. But to speake my iudgement, the inuention, the argument, and the disposition, is not common, nor, (that I know) euer handled of any man before in this order. For the composition and order of

*the verse: Although hee flye not alofte with the winges
of* Astrophell, *nor dare to compare with the Arcadian
shepheard, or any way match with the dainetie Fayry
Queene; yet shall you find his wordes and phrases,
neither Tryuiall nor absurd, but all the whole worke,
for the verse, pleasant, without hardnesse, smooth
without any roughnesse, sweete without tediousnesse,
easie to be vnderstood, without harrish absurdity:
yeelding a gratious harmony euery where, to the delight of the Reader.*

  I haue christened it by the name of Willoby *his*
Auisa: *because I suppose it was his doing, being
written with his owne hand. How he will like my
bouldnes, both in the publishing, and naming of it, I
know not. For the incouraging and helping of maides
and wiues to holde an honest and conastnt course
against all vnhonest and lewd temptations, I haue
doone that I haue doone. I haue not added nor de-
tracted any thing | from the worke it selfe, but* [A2ᵛ
*haue let it passe without altering any thing: Onely in
the end I haue added to fill vp some voyd paper certaine
fragmentes and ditties, as a resolution of a chast and
constant wife, to the tune of Fortune, and the praise of
a contented mind, which I found wrapped altogether
with this, and therefore knew not whether it did any
way belong vnto this or not.*

Thus leauing to trouble your patience with farder delaies. I commit you to the good gouernment of Gods spirit. From my chamber in Oxford this first of October.

Hadrian Dorrell. /   [A3

Abell Emet in commendation of
Willobies Auisa.

*T*O *Willoby, you worthy Dames yeeld worthy prayse,*
Whose siluer pype so sweetly sounds your strange delayes,
Whose lofty style, with golden winges remountes your fame,
The glory of your Princely sex, the spotles name:
O happy wench, who so she be if any be,
That thus deserud thus to be praisd by Willobie,
Shall I beleeue, I must beleeue, such one there is,
Well hast thou said, long maist thou say, such on there is,
If one there be, I can beleeue there are no more,
This wicked age, this sinfull tyme breeds no such store:
Such siluer myntes, such golden mines who could refuse?
Such offers made and not receu'd, I greatly muse.
Such deepe deceit in frendly shewes, such tempting fittes,
To still withstand, doth passe the reach of womens wittes:
You Country maides, Pean nimphes reioyse and sing,
To see from you a chast, a new Diana spring:
At whose report you must not frett, you may not frowne,
But rather stryue by due desert for like renowne,
Her constant faith in hot assaye hath wonne the game,
Whose praise shall liue, when she is dead with lasting fame:
If my conceit from strangers mouth may credit get,
A brauer Theame, more sweetly pend, was neuer yet.

Abell Emet. / [A3*v*]

In praise of Willobie *his* Auisa, *Hex-*ameton to the Author.

*I*N Lauine Land though Liuie bost,
There hath beene seene a Constant *dame:*
Though Rome *lament that she haue lost*
The Gareland *of her rarest fame,*
  Yet now we see, that here is found,
  As great a Faith *in* English *ground.*

Though Collatine *haue deerely bought,*
To high renowne, a lasting life,
And found, that most in vaine haue sought,
To haue a Faire, *and* Constant *wife,*
  Yet Tarquyne *pluckt his glistering grape,*
  And Shake-speare, *paints poore* Lucrece *rape.*

Though Susan *shine in faithfull praise,*
As twinckling Starres in Christall skie,
Penelop's *fame though* Greekes *do raise,*
Of faithfull wiues to make vp three,
  To thinke the Truth, *and say no lesse,*
  Our Auisa *shall make a messe.*

This number knits so sure a knot,
Time *doubtes, that she shall adde no more,*
Vnconstant Nature, *hath begot,*
Of Fleting Feemes, *such fickle store,*
  Two thousand yeares, haue scarcely seene,
  Such as the worst of these haue beene. /   [A 4

Then Aui-Susan *ioyne in one,*
Let Lucres-Auis *be thy name,*
This English Eagle *sores alone,*
And farre surmounts all others fame,
  Where high or low, where great or small,
  This Brytan Bird *out-flies them all.*

Were these three happie, that haue found,
Braue Poets *to depaint their praise?*
Of Rurall Pipe, *with sweetest sound,*
That haue beene heard these many daies,
Sweete wylloby his A V I S blest,
That makes her mount aboue the rest.

Contraria Contrarijs:
Vigilantius: Dormitanus.

Faults escaped.

Folio 8 b staf 2 ver 1 reade bane ver 3 wane Fol 18 a staf 1 ver 2 Soyle staf 4 ve 6 foxly b staf 4 ver 2 and Fol 26 a staf 3 ver 4 foole Fol 27 a staf 3 ver 1 Greece b staf 1 ver 4 strey staf 2 ver 6 fond Fol 28 b staf 1 ver 1 die staf 3 ver 6 from.

WILLOBIE HIS AVISA,

OR

The true picture of a modest Maide,

and of a chast and constant
wife.

CANT. I.

Et martiall men,
   of Mars his praise,
Sound warlike trumpe:
   let lust-led youth,
Of wicked loue,
   write wanton layes;
Let sheepeheards sing,
   their sheepe coates ruth:
The wiser sort,
   confesse it plaine,
That these haue spent good time in vaine.

My sleepie Muse that wakes but now,
Nor now had wak't if one had slept,
To vertues praise hath past her vow,
To paint the Rose which grace hath kept,
   Of sweetest Rose, that still doth spring,
   Of vertues birde my Muse must sing. /   [B 1a

The birde that doth resemble right,
The Turtles faith in constant loue,
The faith that first her promise plight;
No change, nor chance could once remoue:
　　This haue I tri'd; This dare I trust,
　　And sing the truth, I will, I must.

Afflicted *Susans* spotlesse thought,
Intis't by lust to sinfull crime,
To lasting fame her name hath brought,
Whose praise incounters endlesse time:
　　I sing of one whose beauties warre,
　　For trials passe *Susanna's* farre.

The wandring Greekes renowmed mate,
That still withstoode such hote assayes,
Of raging lust whose doubtfull state,
Sought strong refuge, from strange delayes,
　　For fierce assaults and tryals rare,
　　With this my Nimph may not compare.

Hote tryals try where Golde be pure,
The Diamond daunts the sharpest edge,
Light chaffe, fierce flames may not indure,
All quickly leape the lowly hedge,
　　The obiect of my Muse hath past
　　Both force and flame, yet stands she fast.

Though Egle-eyde this bird appeare,
Not blusht at beames of Phœbus raies:
Though Faulkcon wing'd to pearce the aire,
Whose high-pla'st hart no feare dismaies:
   Yet sprang she not from Egles nest,
   But Turtle-bred, loues Turtle best. /   [1*b*

At wester side of Albions Ile,
Where Austine pitcht his Monkish tent,
Where Sheapheards sing, where Muses smile,
The graces met with one consent,
   To frame each one in sundry parte,
   Some cunning worke to shew their arte.

First *Venus* fram'd a luring eye,
A sweete aspect, and comly grace;
There did the Rose and Lillie lie,
That brauely deckt a smiling face,
   Here Cupids mother bent her wil,
   In this to shew her vtmost skill.

Then *Pallas* gaue a reaching head,
With deepe conceites, and passing wit,
A setled mind, not fancie-led,
Abhorring Cupids frantique fit,
   With modest lookes, and blushing cheekes,
   A filed tongue which none mislikes.

Diana deckt the remnant partes
With fewture braue, that nothing lacke,
A quiuer full of pearcing Darts,
She gaue her hanging at her backe;
    And in her hand a Golden shaft,
    To conquer Cupids creeping craft.

This done they come to take the view,
Of nouell worke, of perelesse frame;
Amongst them three, contention grew,
But yet *Diana* gaue the name,
    Auisa shall she called be,
    The chiefe attendant still on me. /   [2 a

When *Iuno* view'd her luring grace,
Olde *Iuno* blusht to see a new,
She fear'd least Ioue would like this face,
And so perhaps might play vntrew,
    They all admir'd so sweete a sight,
    They all enuide so rare a wight.

Beautie
without
riches, is
as a faire
picture
without
life.

When *Iuno* came to giue her wealth,
(Which wanting beautie, wants her life)
She cryde, this face needes not my pelffe,
Great riches sow the seedes of strife:
    I doubt not, some Olympian power
    Will fill her lap, with Golden shower.

This iealous *Iuno* faintly said,
As halfe misdeeming wanton Ioue,
But chast *Diana* tooke the maide,
Such new-bred qualmes quite to remoue:
　　O iealous enuie, filthie beast,
　　For enuie *Iuno* gaue her least.

Iealosie breedes enuy: Both together breed frenzie yet neither of them both can preuaile against wandring fancie.

In lew of *Iun'os* Golden parte,
Diana gaue her double grace;
A chast desire, a constant heart,
Disdaine of loue in fawning face,
　　A face, and eye, that should intice
　　A smile, that should deceiue the wise.

A straunge bayte.

A sober tongue that should allure,
And draw great numbers to the fielde;
A flintie hart, that should indure
All fierce assaults, and neuer yeelde,
　　And seeming oft as though she would;
　　Yet fardest off when that she should. / 　[2*b*

Can filthy sinke yeelde holsome aire,
Or vertue from a vice proceede?
Can enuious hart, or iealous feare
Repell the things that are decreed?
　　By enuie though she lost her thrift,
　　She got by grace a better gift.

Not farre from thence there lyes a vale,
A rosie vale in pleasant plaine;
The Nimphes frequent this happie dale,
Olde Helicon reuiues againe;
   Here Muses sing, here Satyres play,
   Here mirth resounds both night and day.

At East of this, a Castle stands,
By auncient sheepheards built of olde,
And lately was in sheepheards hands,
Though now by brothers bought and solde,
   At west side springs a Christall well;
   There doth this chast *Auisa* dwell.

And there she dwels in publique eye,
Shut vp from none that list to see;
She answeres all that list to try,
Both high and low of each degree:
   But few that come, but feele her dart,
   And try her well ere they depart.

They try'd her hard in hope to gaine,
Her milde behauiour breeds their hope,
Their hope assures them to obtaine,
Till hauing runne their witlesse scope;
   They find their vice by vertue crost,
   Their foolish words, and labour lost. /   [3 *a*

This strange effect, that all should craue,
Yet none obtaine their wrong desire,
A secret gift, that nature gaue,
To feele the frost, amidst the fire:
    Blame not this Dians Nimphe too much,
    Sith God by nature made her such.

Let all the graces now be glad,
That fram'd a grace that past them all,
Let *Iuno* be no longer sad;
Her wanton Ioue hath had a fall;
    Ten yeares haue tryde this constant dame,
    And yet she holds a spotles fame.

Along this plaine there lyes a downe,
Where sheepheards feed their frisking flocke;
Her Sire the Maior of the towne,
A louely shout of auncient stocke,
    Full twentie yeares she liued a maide,
    And neuer was by man betrayde.

At length by *Iuno's* great request,
Diana loth, yet gaue her leaue,
Of flowring yeares, to spend the rest
In wed-locke band; but yet receiue,   A good gift.
    Quod she, this gift; Thou virgin pure,
    Chast wife in wed-locke shalt indure.

O happie man that shall enioy
A blessing of so rare a price;
That frees the hart from such annoy;
As often doth torment the wise,
   A louing wife vnto her death,
   With full assurance of her faith. | [3 ^b

When flying fame began to tell,
How beauties wonder was returnd,
From countrie hils, in towne to dwell,
With special gifts and grace adornd,
   Of sutors store there might you see;
   And some were men, of high degree.

But wisdom wild her chuse her mate,
If that she lou'd a happy life,
That might be equall to her state,
To crop the sprigges of future strife;
   Where rich in grace, wher sound in health,
   Most men do wed, but for the wealth.

Though iealous *Iuno* had denyde
This happy wench, great store of pelffe:
Yet is she now in wedlocke tyde,
To one that loues her as himselfe,
   So thus they liue, and thus they loue;
   And God doth blesse them from aboue.

This rare seene bird, this Phœnix sage
Yeelds matter to my drowsie pen,
The mirror of this sinneful age,
That giues vs beasts in shapes of men,
　　Such beasts as still continue sinne,
　　Where age doth leaue, there youths begin.

Our English soile, to Sodoms sinke
Excessiue sinne transformd of late,
Of foule deceite the lothsome linke,
Hath worne all faith cleane out of date,
　　The greatest sinnes mongst greatest sort,
　　Are counted now but for a sport. /　　　[4a

Old Asues grandame is restor'd;
Her grouie Caues are new refinde:　　　2. Chro.
The monster Idoll is ador'd　　　　　　15. 16
By lustie dames of Macha's kinde:
　　They may not let this worship fall,
　　Although they leese their honours all.

Our Moab Cozbies cast no feare,
To let in view of euery eye,　　　　　　Numer.
Their gainelesse games they holde so deere,　25. 6.
They follow must, although they dye.
　　For why? the sword that Phineas wore,
　　Is broken now, and cuts no more.

My tender Muse, that neuer try'd
Her ioynted wings till present time,
At first the perelesse bird espy'd,
That mounts aloft, deuoide of crime;
　　Though high she sore, yet will I trie,
　　Where I her passage can discry.

Her high conceites, her constant minde;
Her sober talke, her stout denies;
Her chast aduise, here shall you find;
Her fierce assaults, her milde replies,
　　Her dayly fight with great and small,
　　Yet constant vertue conquers all.

The first that saies to plucke the Rose,
That scarce appear'd without the bud,
With Gorgeous shewes of Golden glose,
To sow the seeds that were not good:
　　Suppose it were some noble man
　　That tride her thus, and thus began. / [4*b*

The first triall of AVISA, before

she was married, by a Noble man: vnder

which is represented a warning to all young maids
of euery degree, that they beware of the alluring intisements of great
men.

CANT. II.

Ow is the time,
   if thou be wise,
Thou happie maide,
   if thou canst see,
Thy happiest time,
   take good aduise,
Good fortune laughs,
   be rulde by me:
Be rulde by me,
   and her's my faith,
No Golde shall want thee till thy death.

NOB.

Thou knowest my power, thou seest my might,
Thou knowest I can maintaine thee well,
And helpe thy friends vnto their right;
Thou shalt with me for euer dwell,
   My secret friend thou shalt remaine,
   And all shall turne to thy great gaine.

Thou seest thy parents meane estate,
That barres the hope of greater chance;
And if thou proue not wise too late,
Thou maist thy selfe, and thine aduance:
   Repulse not fondly this good hap,
    That now lies offred in thy lap. /   [C5*a*

Abandon feare that bars consent,
Repel the shame that feares a blot,
Let wisdome way what faith is ment,
That all may praise thy happie lot;
    Thinke not I seeke thy liues disgrace;
    For thou shalt haue a Ladies place.

Thou art the first my fancie chose,
I know thy friends will like it well:
This friendly fault to none disclose,
And what thou thinkst, blush not to tell,
    Thou seest my loue, thou know'st my mind,
    Now let me feele, what grace I find.

CANT. III.

AVISA   YOur Honours place, your riper yeares,
      Might better frame some grauer talkes:
Midst sunnie rayes, this cloud appeares;
Sweete Roses grow on prickly stalkes:
    If I conceiue, what you request,
    You aime at that I most detest.

My tender age that wants aduice,
And craues the aide of sager guides,
Should rather learne for to be wise,
To stay my steps from slipperie slides;
    Then thus to sucke, then thus to tast
    The poys'ned sap, that kils at last.

I wonder what your wisdome ment,
Thus to assault a silly maide:
Some simple wench, might chance consent,
By false resembling shewes betraide:
    I haue by grace a natiue shield,
    To lewd assaults that cannot yeeld, /   [5b

I am too base to be your wife,
You choose me for your secret frend;
That is to lead a filthy life,
Whereon attends a fearefull end:
    Though I be poore, I tell you plaine,
    To be your whore, I flat disdaine.

Your high estate, your siluer shrines,
Repleate with wind and filthy stinke;
Your glittering gifts, your golden mynes,
May force some fooles perhaps to shrinke:
    But I haue learnd that sweetest bayt,
    Oft shrowds the hooke of most desayt.

C

What great good hap, what happie time,
Your proffer brings, let yeelding maids
Of former age, which thought to clime,
To highest tops of earthly aids,
    Come backe a while, and let them tell,
    Where wicked liues haue ended well.

Shores wife, a Princes secret frend,
Faire *Rosomond*, a Kings delight:
Yet both haue found a gastly end,
And fortunes friends, felt fortunes spight:
    What greater ioyes, could fancie frame,
    Yet now we see, their lasting shame.

If princely pallace haue no power,
To shade the shame of secret sinne,
If blacke reproch such names deuoure,
What gaine, or glory can they winne,
    That tracing tracts of shamelesse trade,
    A hate of God, and man are made? /   [6*a*

This onely vertue must aduaunce
My meane estate to ioyfull blisse:
For she that swaies dame vertues launce,
Of happie state can neuer misse,
    But they that hope to gaine by vice,
    Shall surely proue too late vnwise.

The roote of woe is fond desire,
That neuer feeles her selfe content:
But wanton wing'd, will needes aspire,
To finde the thing, she may lament,
  A courtly state, a Ladies place,
  My former life will quite deface.

Such strange conceites may hap preuaile,
With such as loue such strong desayts,
But I am taught such qualmes to quaile,
And flee such sweete alluring bayts,
  The witlesse Flie playes with the flame,
  Till she be scorched with the same.

You long to know what grace you find,
In me, perchance, more then you would,
Except you quickly change your mind,
I find in you, lesse then I should,
  Moue this no more, vse no reply,
  I'le keepe mine honour till I die.

CANT. IIII.

ALas, good soule, and will yee so?   N O B.
  You will be chast *Diana's* mate;
Till time haue woue the web of woe,
Then to repent wil be too late,
  You shew your selfe so foole-precise,
  That I can hardly thinke you wise, /   [6b

You sprang belike from Noble stocke,
That stand so much vpon your fame,
You hope to stay vpon the rocke,
That will preserue a faultlesse name,
    But while you hunt for needelesse praise,
    You loose the Prime of sweetest daies.

A merry time, when countrie maides
Shall stand (forsooth) vpon their garde;
And dare controll the Courtiers deedes,
At honours gate that watch and warde;
    When Milke maids shal their pleasures flie,
    And on their credits must relie.

Ah silly wench, take not a pride,
Though thou my raging fancie moue,
Thy betters far, if they were try'd,
Would faine accept my proffered loue;
    T'was for thy good, if thou hadst wist,
    For I may haue whome ere I list.

But here thy folly may appeare,
Art thou preciser then a Queene:
Cornelius Agrippa. Queene *Ioane* of Naples did not feare,
To quite mens loue, with loue againe:
    And *Messalina*, t'is no newes,
    Was dayly seene to haunt the stewes.

And *Cleopatra*, prince of Nile,
With more then one was wont to play:
And yet she keepes her glorious stile,
And fame that neuer shall decaie,
    What need'st thou then to feare of shame,
    When Queenes and Nobles vse the same?/[7 *a*

CANT. V.

N Eeds must the sheepe strake all awrie,   *AVISA*
    Whose sheepheards wander from their way:
Needes must the sickly patient die,
Whose Doctor seekes his liues decay:
    Needs must the people well be taught,
    Whose chiefest leaders all are naught.

Such lawlesse guides Gods people found,
When Moab maides allur'd their fall;
They sought no salue to cure this wound,
Till God commaunds, to hange them all;
    For wicked life, a shamefull end
    To wretched men, the Lord doth send.

Was earth consumde with wreakfull waues?
Did Sodom burne and after sinke?
What sinne is that, which vengaunce craues;
If wicked lust no sinne we thinke?
    O blind conceites! O filthy breath!
    That drawes vs headlong to our death.

If death be due to euery sinne,
How can I then be too precise?
Where pleasures end, if paine beginne,
What neede haue we, then to be wise?
   They weaue indeed the web of woe,
   That from the Lord doe yeeld to goe.

I will remember whence I came,
I hunt not for this worldly praise,
I long to keepe a blamelesse fame,
And constant hart gainst hard assaies:
   If this be folly, want of skill,
   I will remaine thus foolish still. /   [7b

The blindfold rage of Heathen Queenes,
Or rather queanes that know not God,
Gods heauie iudgements tried since,
And felt the waight of angry rod;
   God saue me from that Sodomes crie,
   Whose deadly sting shall neuer die.

CANT. VI.

N O B.

FOrgiue me wench, I did mistake,
  I little thought, that you could preach,
  All worldly ioyes, you must forsake:
For so your great Diuines doe teach,
   But yet beware, be not too bold,
   A yongling Saint, a Deuill old.

Well wanton well, thou art but yong,
This is the error of thy youth,
Thou wilt repent this faith ere long,
And see too late (perhaps) the truth;
    And they that seeme so pure at first,
    Are often found in proofe the worst.

Thy youth and beautie will not last,
For sicknes one, the other age
May captiue take, when both are past,
You may haue leasure to be sage,
    The time will come, if these retire,
    The worst will scorne that I desire.

Of chast renowme, you seeke the praise,
You build your hope aboue the ayre,
When wonders last not twentie daies,
What need you rusticke rumors feare?
    Esteeme not words aboue thy wealth,
    Which must procure thy credits health. / [8 a

And yet in truth I can not see,
From whence such great discredit growes,
To liue in spight of euery eye,
And swim in silkes, and brauest shewes,
    To take the choise of daintiest meate,
    And see thy betters stand and waite.

These graue respects breede pleasures braue,
Thy youthly yeares for ioyes craue,
And fading credit hath his waue,
That none to thee doth shine so braue:
　　That smokie fame which likes thee best,
　　The wisest haue esteemed least.

CANT. VII.

AVISA

WEll now I see, why Christ commends,
　To louing mates the Serpents wit,
That stops his eares, and so defends
His hart, from luring sounds vnfit,
　　If you your madnes still bewraye,
　　I'le stop my eares, or goe my way.

Vlisses wise, yet dar'd not stay
The tising sound of Syrens song:
What fancie then doth me betray,
That thinke my selfe, so wise and strong;
　　That dare to heare, what you dare speake,
　　And hope for strength, when you be weake?

My wisdome is the liuing Lord,
That giues me grace which nature wants,
That holds my seate from waies abhord,
And in my hart good motions plants:
　　With him I dare to bide the field,
　　Striue while you list, I can not yeeld. /　[8*b*

Fond fauour failes, the time will passe,
All earthly pleasures haue their end,
We see not that, which sometime was,
Nor that which future times will send:
    You say the truth, remember this,
    And then confesse, you stray amisse.

The shorter time, the greater care,
Are pleasures vaine? the lesse delight,
Are daungers nye? why then beware,
From base affections take your flight,
    Thinke God a reckning will require,
    And striue to quaile this bad desire.

To swim in silkes, and braue aray,
Is that you thinke which women loue,
That leads poore maides so oft astray,
That are not garded from aboue?
    But this I know, that know not all,
    Such wicked pride, will haue a fall.

CANT. VIII.

N O B.

Las the feare, alas the fall,
And what's the fall, that you so feare?
To tosse good fortunes golden ball,
And gaine the goale I prize so deare,
  I doubt least these your needlesse feares,
  Will bar good hap, from witlesse yeares./ [D9a

Thy age experience wants I see,
And lacking tryall art afraid,
Least ventring farre to credit me,
Our secret dealings might be wrayd;
  What then doth not my mightie name,
  Suffice to sheeld thy fact from shame?

Who dare to stirre, who dares to speake,
Who dares our dealings to reproue?
Though some suspect, yet none will creake,
Or once controll thy worthy loue;
  My might will stand for thy defence,
  And quite thee cleare from great offence.

Who see our face, knowes not our facts,
Though we our sport in secret vse,
Thy cheekes will not bewray thy acts,
But rather blushing make excuse:
    If thou wilt yeeld, here is my faith,
    I'le keepe it secret till thy death.

To seeme as chast, let that suffice,
Although indeed thou be not so,
Thus deale our women that are wise,
And let thy godly Doctors go,
    Still faine as though thou godly art,
    It is inough, who knowes thy hart?

Let not the idle vulgar voice,
Of fained credit witch thee so,
To force thee leaue this happie choise,
And flying pleasure liue in woe;
    If thou refuse, assure thy mind,
    The like of this shalt neuer find. /   [9*b*

CANT. IX.

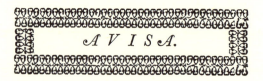

AVISA.

L Et that word stand, let that be true,
  I doe refuse and so doe still,
God shield me from your cursed crew,
That thus are led by beastly will,
    It grieues my hart, that I doe find
    In Noble bloud so base a mind.

On worldly feare, you thinke I stand,
Or fame that may my shame resound,
No Sir, I feare his mightie hand,
That will both you and me confound,
    His feare it is that makes me stay
    My wandring steps from wicked way.

Who dares, say you, our facts vnfold?
Eu'n he that can mightie Kings tame,
And he that Princes hath controld,
He dares prouide a mightie shame,
    What fence haue you for to withstand
    His firie plagues, and heuie hand?

Though *Samson* queld the Lyons rage,
Though *Solomon*, a mightie King,
Yet when to sinne their harts they gage,
On both doth God confusion bring,
    How can you then his wrath auoid,
    That you and yours be not destroid? /   [10a

He sees our facts, he viewes our deeds,
Although we sinne in secret place,
A guiltie conscience alwaies bleeds:
My faults will shew vpon my face,
    My cheekes will blush, when I doe sin;
    Let all men know, when I begin.

To seeme as chast, and not to be,
To beare a shew, and yet to faine,
Is this the loue, you beare to me,
To damne my soule in lasting paine?
    If this the best you haue to say,
    Pray giue me leaue, to goe my way.

CANT. X.

NOB.

WEll then I see, you haue decreed,
    And this decree must light on mee:
Vnhappie Lillie loues a weed,
That giues no sent, that yeelds no glee,
    Thou art the first I euer tride,
    Shall I at first be thus denide?

My haplesse hap, fell much awrie,
To fix my fancies prime delight,
In haggard Hauke that mounts so hie,
That checkes the lure, and Fawkners sight;
    But sore you hie, or flie you low,
    Stoupe needs you must, before you goe. / [10*b*

Your modest speech is not amisse,
Your maidens blush becomes you well;
Now will I see how sweete you kisse,
And so my purpose farder tell;
    Your coye lookes and trickes are vaine,
    I will no nay, and that is plaine.

Thou must perforce be well content,
To let me win thee with thy will;
Thy chiefest friends haue giu'n consent,
And therefore thinke, it is not ill,
　　Abandon all thy fond delay;
　　And marke this well, that I shall say.

My house, my hart, my land my life,
My credit to thy care I giue:
And if thou list to be a wife,
In shew of honest fame to liue;
　　I'le fit thee one, shall beare the cloke,
　　And be a chimnie for the smoke.

But say the word, it shall be don,
And what thou list, or what thou craue,
What so be lost, what euer won,
Shall nothing want, that thou wilt haue,
　　Thou shalt haue all, what wilt thou more,
　　Which neuer woman had before.

Here's fortie Angels to begin;
A little pledge of great goodwill,
To buy thee lace, to buy a pin;
I will be carefull of thee still:
　　If youth be quaild, if I be old,
　　I can supply that with my gold. /　　[11a

Silke gownes and veluet shalt thou haue,
With hoods and cauls, fit for thy head;
Of goldsmithes worke a border braue,
A chaine of golde ten double spread;
   And all the rest shall answere this,
   My purse shall see that nothing misse.

Two wayting maides, attendant still,
Two seruing men, foure geldings prest,
Go where you list, ride where you will,
No iealous thought shal me molest;
   Two hundreth pounds I doe intend,
   To giue thee yearely for to spend.

Of this I will assurance make,
To some good friend, whom thou wilt chuse
That this in trust from me shall take,
While thou dost liue, vnto thy vse;
   A thousand markes, to thee giue I,
   And all my Iewels when I die.

This will I doe, what euer chance,
I'le shortly send, and fetch thee hence;
Thy chiefest friends I will aduance,
And leaue them cause of no offence,
   For all this same, I onely craue
   But thy good-will, that let me haue.

A modest maide is loth to say,
In open words, she doth consent,
Till gentle force doe breake the stay,
Come on mine owne, and be content,
   Possesse me of my loues desire,
   And let me tast that I require. /   [11*b*

CANT. XI.

AVISA.

H And off my Lord, this will not serve,
  Your wisdome wanders much awrie,
From reasons rule thus farre to swarue,
I'le neuer yeeld, I'le rather die,
   Except you leaue, and so depart,
   This knife shall sticke within your hart.

Is this the loue, your franticke fit
Did so pretend in glosing shew?
Are these your waies, is this your wit,
To tice and force poore maidens so?
   You striue in vaine, by raging lust,
   To gaine consent, or make me trust.

D

For who can trust your flattering stile,
Your painted words, your braue pretence,
When you will striue, by trayned will
To force consent to lewd offence,
   Then thus to yeeld by chaunted charmes,
   I'le rather die within your armes.

Your golden Angels I repell,
Your lawlesse lust I here defie
These Angels are the posts of hell,
That often lead poore soules awrie,
   Shame on them all, your eyes shall see,
   These Angels haue no power of me. / '[12a

Your gownes of silke, your golden chaines,
Your men, your maides, your hundreth pounds,
Are nothing else but diuelish traines,
That fill fond eares with tickling sounds,
   A bladder full of traiterous wind,
   And fardest off from filthy mind.

Well, sith your meaning now is plaine,
And lust would giue no longer leaue,
To faithlesse hart, to lie and faine,
Which might perchance in time deceiue,
   By Iesus Christ I doe protest,
   I'le neuer graunt that you request.

CANT. XII.

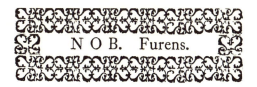

N O B.   Furens.

THou beggers brat, thou dunghill mate,
  Thou clownish spawne, thou country gill,
My loue is turnd to wreakefull hate,
Go hang, and keepe thy credit still,
    Gad where thou list, aright or wrong,
    I hope to see thee begge, erre long.

Was this great offer well refus'd,
Or was this proffer all too base?
Am I fit man to be abus'd,
With such disgrace, by flattering gase?
    On thee or thine, as I am man,
    I will reuenge this if I can. /   [12*b*

Thou think'st thy selfe a pearelesse peice,
And peeuish pride that doth possesse
Thy hart; perswades that thou art wise,
When God doth know ther's nothing lesse,
    T'was not thy beautie that did moue
    This fond affect, but blinded loue.

I hope to see some countrie clowne,
Possessor of that fleering face,
When need shall force thy pride come downe,
I'le laugh to see thy foolish case,
    For thou that think'st thy selfe so braue,
    Wilt take at last some paltrie knaue,

Thou selfewill gig that dost detest
My faithfull loue, looke to thy fame,
If thou offend, I doe protest,
I'le bring thee out to open shame,
    For sith thou fayn'st thy selfe so pure,
    Looke to thy leapes that they be sure.

I was thy friend, but now thy foe,
Thou hadst my hart, but now my hate,
Refusing wealth, God send thee woe,
Repentance now will come too late,
    That tongue that did protest my faith,
    Shall waile thy pride, and wish thy death./[E13a

CANT. XIII.

YEa so I thought, this is the end
Of wandring lust, resembling loue,
Wa'st loue or lust, that did intend
Such friendlesse force, as you did moue?
    Though you may vaunt of happier fate,
    I am content with my estate.

I rather chuse a quiet mind,
A conscience cleare from bloudy sinnes,
Then short delights, and therein find
That gnawing worme, that neuer linnes,
    Your bitter speeches please me more,
    Then all your wealth, and all your store.

I loue to liue deuoid of crime,
Although I begge, although I pine,
These fading ioyes for little time,
Imbrace who list, I here resine,
    How poore I goe, how meane I fare,
    If God be pleas'd, I doe not care.

I rather beare your raging ire,
Although you sweare reuengment deepe,
Then yeeld for gaine to lewd desire,
That you might laugh, when I should weepe,
   Your lust would like but for a space,
   But who could salue my foule disgrace?/ [13 *b*

Mine eares haue heard your taunting words,
Of yeelding fooles by you betraid,
Amongst your mates at open bords,
Know'st such a wife? know'st such a maid?
   Then must you laugh, then must you winke,
   And leaue the rest for them to thinke.

Nay yet welfare the happie life,
That need not blush at euery view:
Although I be a poore mans wife,
Yet then I'le laugh as well as you,
   Then laugh as long, as you thinke best,
   My fact shall frame you no such iest.

If I doe hap to leape aside,
I must not come to you for aide,
Alas now that you be denide,
You thinke to make me sore afraide;
   Nay watch your worst, I doe not care,
   If I offend, pray doe not spare.

You were my friend, you were but dust,
The Lord is he, whome I doe loue,
He hath my hart, in him I trust,
And he doth gard me from aboue,
    I waie not death, I feare not hell,
    This is enough, and so farewell. /   [14a

THE SECOND TEMP-
tation of AVISA, after her marri-

age by Ruffians, Roysters, young
Gentlemen, and lustie Captaines, which all shee
quickly cuts off.

CANT. XIIII.

CAVEILEIRO.

Ome lustie wench,
I like thy lookes,
And such a pleasant
looke I loue,
Thine eyes are like
to bayted hookes,
That force the hungrie
fish to moue,
Where nature granteth
such a face,
I need not doubt to purchase grace.

I doubt not but thy inward thought,
Doth yeeld as fast as doth thine eye;
A loue in me hath fancie wrought,
Which worke you can not well denye;
    From loue you can not me refraine,
    I seeke but this, loue me againe. /   [14 *b*

And so thou dost, I know it well,
I knew it by thy side-cast glance,
Can hart from outwood looke rebell?
Which yeaster night I spide by chance;
    Thy loue (sweete hart) shall not be lost,
    How deare a price so euer it cost.

Aske what thou wilt, thou know'st my mind,
Appoint the place, and I will come,
Appoint the time, and thou shalt find,
Thou canst not fare so well at home,
    Few words suffice, where harts consent,
    I hope thou know'st, and art content.

Though I a stranger seeme as yet,
And seldome seene, before this day,
Assure thy selfe that thou mayst get,
More knackes by me, then I will say,
    Such store of wealth as I will bring,
    Shall make thee leape, shal make thee sing,

I must be gone, vse no delay,
At six or seuen the chance may rise,
Old gamesters know their vantage play,
And when t'is best to cast the dice,
　　Leaue ope your poynt, take vp your man,
　　And mine shall quickly enter than.

CANT. XV,

A V I S A.

/[15*a*

WHat now? what newes? new warres in hand?
　　More trumpets blowne of fond conceites?
More banners spread of follies band?
New Captaines coyning new deceites?
　　Ah woe is me, new campes are pla'st,
　　Whereas I thought all daungers past.

O wretched soule, what face haue I,
That can not looke, but some misdeame?
What sprite doth lurke within mine eye,
That kendles thoughts so much vncleane?
　　O lucklesse fewture neuer blest,
　　That sow'st the seedes of such vnrest.

What wandring fits are these that moue
Your hart, inragde with euery glance;
That iudge a woman straight in loue,
That welds her eye aside by chance,
    If this your hope, by fancie wrought,
    You hope on that, I neuer thought.

If nature giue me such a looke,
Which seemes at first vnchast or ill,
Yet shall it proue no bayted hooke,
To draw your lust to wanton will,
    My face and will doe not agree,
    Which you in time (perhaps) may see.

If smiling cheare and friendly words,
If pleasant talke such thoughts procure,
Yet know my hart, no will afords,
To scratching kites, to cast the lure,
    If milde behauvior thus offend,
    I will assaie this fault to mend. /   [15*b*

You plant your hope vpon the sand,
That build on womens words, or smiles;
For when you thinke your selfe to stand
In greatest grace, they proue but wyles,
    When fixt you thinke on surest ground,
    Then fardest off they will be found.

CANT. XVI,

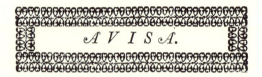

AVISA.

YOu speake of loue, you talke of cost,
  Is't filthy loue your worship meanes?
Assure your selfe your labor's lost;
Bestow your cost among your queanes,
    You left not here, nor here shall find,
    Such mates as match your beastly mind.

You must againe to Coleman hedge,
For there be some that looke for gaine,
They will bestow the French mans badge,
In lew of all your cost and paine,
    But Sir, it is against my vse,
    For gaine to make my house a stewes.

What haue you seene, what haue I doon,
That you should iudge my mind so light,
That I so quickly might be woon,
Of one that came but yeaster night?
    Of one I wist not whence he came,
    Nor what he is, nor what's his name?/ [16*a*

Though face doe friendly smile on all,
Yet iudge me not to be so kind,
To come at euery Faulkners call,
Or waue aloft with euery wind,
    And you that venter thus to try,
    Shall find how far you shoote awry.

And if your face might be your iudge,
Your wannie cheekes, your shaggie lockes,
Would rather moue my mind to grudge,
To feare the piles, or else the pockes:
    Yf you be mou'd, to make amends,
    Pray keepe your knackes for other frends.

You may be walking when you list,
Looke ther's the doore, and ther's the way,
I hope you haue your market mist,
Your game is lost, for lacke of play,
    The point is close, no chance can fall,
    That enters there, or euer shall.

CANT. XVII.

CAVELEIRO.

GOds wo: I thinke you doe but iest,
  You can not thus delude my hope:

A right
Caueleiro.

But yet perhaps you thinke it best,
  At first to giue but little scope:
    At first assault you must retire,
    And then be fors't to yeeld desire. /   [16b

You thinke, that I would iudge you bad,
If you should yeeld at first assaie,
And you may thinke me worse then mad,
If on repulse send me awaie,
  You thinke you doe your credit wrong,
  Except you keepe your sutors long.

But I that know the wonted guise,
Of such as liue in such a place,
Old dame experience makes me wise,
To know your meaning by your face,
  For most of them, that seeme so chast,
  Denie at first, and take at last.

This painted sheth, may please some foole,
That can not see the rustie knife:
But I haue bin too long at schooles,
To thinke you of so pure a life,
    The time and place will not permit,
    That you can long, here spot-lesse sit.

And therefore wench, be not so strange,
To grant me that, which others haue,
I know that women loue to change,
T''is but deceite, to seeme so graue,
    I neuer haue that woman tri'd,
    Of whome as yet I was deni'd.

Your godly zeale doth breed my trust,
Your anger makes me hope the more;
For they are often found the worst,
That of their conscience make such store,
    In vaine to blush, or looke aside,
    A flat repulse, I can not bide. /   [F 1 7 *a*

CANT. XVIII.

AVISA.

THou wicked wretch, what dost not thinke
There is a God that doth behold
This sinnefull waies, this Sodoms sinke?
O wretched earth that art so bold,
　To iest at God, and at his word,
　Looke for his iust reuenging sword.

1. Cor. 5.　Saint Paul commands vs not to eate,
With him that leads a wicked life;
Or shall be found to lie in waite,
To seeke to spoyle his neighbours wife,
Reuela.　　Such wicked soules God doth forsake,
12.　　　And dings them downe to fierie lake.

A young
man was
striken
blind for
looking
dis-
honestly
vpon a
godly wo-
man.

A brain-sicke youth was striken blind,
That sent his greedie eye to view,
A godly wench, with godlesse mind,
That paine might spring, whence pleasures grew,
　Remember friend, forget not this,
　And see you looke no more amisse.

The Locrenses vse to put out both the eyes of the adulterers.

O *Iulia* flower of thy time,
Where is thy law, where is thy word,
That did condemne the wedlocke crime,
To present death, with bloudy sword?
 The shining of this percing edge,
 Would daunt the force of filthy rage. / [17b

The law
Iulia in
Rome put
adulterers
to the
sword.
The Ara-
bians doe
the like.

Though shamelesse Callets may be found;
That oyle them selues in common field;
And can carire the whoores rebound,
To straine at first, and after yeeld:
 Yet here are none of *Creseds* kind,
 In whome you shall such fleeting find.

The time and place may not condemne,
The mind to vice that doth not sway,
But they that vertue doe condemne,
By time and place, are led astray,
 This place doth hold on at this time,
 That will not yeeld to bloudy crime.

You thinke that others haue possest
The place that you so lewdly craue,
Wherein you plainely haue confest,
Your selfe to be a iealous knaue,
 The rose vnblusht hath yet no staine,
 Nor euer shall, while I remaine.

E

CANT- XIX.

CAVELEIRO.

MEthinkes I heare a sober Fox,
Stand preaching to the gagling Geese;
And shewes them out a painted box,
And bids them all beware of cheese,
    Your painted box, and goodly preach,
    I see doth hold a boxly reach. /   [18a

Perchance you be no common card,
But loue the daintie diamonds place,
The ten, the knaue, may be your gard,
Yet onely you, are still the ace,
    Contented close in packe to lie,
    But open dealing you defie.

Well I confesse, I did offend,
To rush so headlong to the marke;
Yet giue me leaue this fault to mend,
And craue your pardon in the darke,
    Your credits fame I will not spill,
    But come as secret as you will.

Nay her's my hand, my faith I giue,
My tongue my fact shall not reueale,
To earthly creature while I liue;
Because you loue a secret deale,
   And where I come, I still will say,
   She would not yeeld, but said me nay.

So shall your credit greater grow,
By my report a passing praise
And they that scant your name doe know,
Your fame on hie, and hie shall raise,
   So shall you gaine that you desire,
   By granting that, which I require.

To plant a siege, and yet depart,
Before the towne be yeelded quite,
It kils a martiall manly hart,
That can not brooke such high despite,
   Then say you yea, or say you no,
   I'le scale your wals, before I go. /   [18b

CANT. XX.

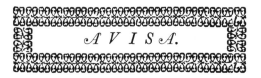

A V I S A.

A Fine deuice, and well contriu'd,
  Braue Golde vpon a bitter pill;
No maruaile well though you haue thriu'd,
That so can decke, that so can dill;
    Your quaintish quirkes can want no mate;
    But here I wis, you come too late.

It's ill to hault before the lame,
Or watch the bird that can not sleepe,
Your new found trickes are out of frame,
The fox will laugh, when Asses weepe;
    Sweare what you list, say what you will,
    Before you spake, I knew your skill.

Your secret dealing will not hold,
To force me trie, or make me trust
Your blind deuises are too old,
Your broken blade hath got the rust,
    You need not lie, but truely say,
    She would not yeeld to wanton play.

Your tongue shall spare to spread my fame,
I list not buy too deare a sound,
Your greatest praise would breed but shame,
Report of me, as you haue found,
    Though you be loth to blow retreat,
    This mount's too strong for you to get. / [19*a*

The wisest Captaine now and then,
When that he feeles his foe too strong;
Retires betime to saue his men,
That grow but weake, if seege be long;
    From this assault you may retire,
    You shall not reach, that you require.

I hate to feede you with delaies,
As others doe, that meane to yeeld,
You spend in vaine your strong assaies,
To win the towne, or gaine the feeld;
    No Captaine did, nor euer shall,
    Set ladder here, to skale the wall.

CANT XXI.

CAVELEIRO.

HAd I knowne this when I began,
    You would haue vsde me as you say,
I would haue take you napping than,
And giue you leaue to say me nay,
    I little thought to find you so:
    I neuer dreamt, you would say no.

Such selfe like wench I neuer met,
Great cause haue I thus hard to craue it,
If euer man haue had it yet, /   [19*b*
I sworen haue, that I will haue it,
    If thou didst neuer giue consent;
    I must perforce, be then content.

If thou wilt sweare, that thou hast knowne,
In carnall act, no other man:
But onely one, and he thine owne,
Since man and wife you first began,
    I'le leaue my sute, and sweare it trew,
    Thy like in deed, I neuer knew.

CANT. XXII.

A V I S A.

I Told you first what you should find,
  Although you thought I did but iest,
And selfe affection made you blind,
To seeke the thing, I most detest;
    Besides his host, who takes the paine,
    To recken first, must count againe.

Your rash swore oth you must repent,
You must beware of headlong vowes;
Excepting him, whome free consent,
By wedlocke words, hath made my spouse,
    From others yet I am as free,
    As they this night, that boren bee. / [20a

CAVELEIRO.

WEll giue me then a cup of wine,
As thou art his, would thou were mine.

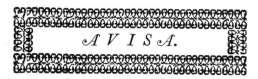

AVISA.

HAue t'ye good-lucke, tell them that gaue
You this aduice, what speede you haue.

Farewell.

/ [20*b*

The third trial; wherin are expressed the long
passionate, and constant affections of the close and
wary sutor, which by signes, by sighes, by letters, by pri-
uie messengers, by Iewels, Rings, Golde, diuers gifts, and by
a long continued course of courtesie, at length pre-
uaileth with many both maides and wiues, if they be not
garded wounderfully with a better spirite
then their owne, which all are here
finely daunted, and mildly o-
uer throwne, by the constant
aunsweres, and chast
replies of Auisa.

CANT. XXIII.

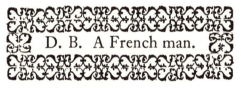

D. B. A French man.

S flaming flakes,
　　too closely pent,
With smothering smoke,
　　in narrow vault,
Each hole doth trie,
　　to get a vent,
And force by forces,
　　fierce assault,
With ratling rage,
　　doth rumbling raue,
Till flame and smoke free passage haue. / [G21a

So I (my deare) haue smothered long,
Within my hart a sparkling flame,
Whose rebell rage is grown so strong,
That hope is past to quell the same,
    Except the stone, that strake the fire,
    With water quench this hote desire.

The glauncing speare, that made the wound,
Which ranckling thus, hath bred my paine,
Must pearcing slide with fresh rebound,
And wound, with wound, recure againe.
    That flooting eye that pearst my hart,
    Must yeeld to salue my curelesse smart.

I striu'd, but striu'd against the streame,
To daunt the qualmes of fond desire,
The more their course I did restraine,
More strong and strong they did retire,
    Bare need doth force me now to runne,
    To seeke my helpe, where hurt begunne.

Thy present state wants present aid,
A quicke redresse my griefe requires,
Let not the meanes be long delaid,
That yeelds vs both our harts desires,
    If you will ease my pensiue hart,
    I'le find a salue to heale your smart.

I am no common gameling mate,
That list to bowle in euery plaine,
But (wench) consider both our state,
The time is now, for both to gaine,
    From daungerous bands I set you free,
    If you wil yeeld to comfort mee. /   [21b

CANT. XXIIII.

AVISA.

Your fierie flame, your secret smart,
    That inward frets with pining griefe,
    Your hollow sighes, your heuie hart,
Methinks might quickly find reliefe,
    If once the certaine cause were knowne,
    From whence these hard effects haue growne.

It little boots to shew your sore,
To her that wants all Phisicke skill,
But tell it them, that haue in store,
Such oyles as creeping cankers kill,
    I would be glad, to doe my best,
    If I had skill, to giue you rest.

Take heede, let not your griefe remaine,
Till helpes doe faile, and hope be past,
For such as first refus'd some paine,
A double paine haue felt at last,
   A little sparke, not quencht be time,
   To hideous flames will quickly clime.

If godly sorrow for your sin,
Be chiefest cause, why you lament,
If giltie conscience doe begin,
To draw you truely to repent,
   A ioyfull end must needs redound,
   To happie griefe so seldome found. /   [22a

To striue all wicked lusts to quell,
Which often sort to dolefull end,
I ioye to heare you meane so well,
And what you want, the Lord will send:
   But if you yeeld to wanton will,
   God will depart, and leaue you still.

Your pleasant aide with sweete supply,
My present state, that might amend,
If honest loue be ment thereby,
I shall be glad of such a frend,
   But if you loue, as I suspect,
   Your loue and you, I both reiect.

CANT. XXV.

D. B. A French man.

WHat you suspect, I can not tell,
     What I doe meane, you may perceiue,
     My workes shall shew, I wish you well,
If well ment loue you list receiue,
   I haue beene long in secret mind,
   And would be still your secret frind.

My loue should breed you no disgrace,
None should perceiue our secret plaie,
We would obserue both time and place,
That none our dealings should bewraie,
   Be it my fortune, or my fault,
   Loue makes me venter this assault. /   [22*b*

You mistresse of my doubtfull chance,
You Prince of this my soules desire,
That lulls my fancie in a trance,
The marke whereto my hopes aspire,
   You see the sore, whence springs my griefe
   You weld the sterne of my reliefe.

The grauest men of former time,
That liu'd with fame, and happie life,
Haue thought it none, or pettie crime,
To loue a friend besides their wife,
    Then sith my wife you can not be,
    As dearest friend accompt of me.

You talke of sinne, and who doth liue,
Whose dayly steps slide not awrie?
But too precise, doth deadly grieue,
The hart that yeelds not yet to die,
    When age drawes on, and youth is past,
    Then let vs thinke of this at last.

The Lord did loue King *Dauid* well,
Although he had more wiues then one:
King *Solomon* that did excell,
For wealth and wit, yet he alone,
    A thousand wiues and friends possest,
    Yet did he thriue, yet was he blest.

CANT. XXVI.

A V I S A.

/[23a

O Mightie Lord, that guides the Spheare;
  Defend me by thy mightie will,
From iust reproch, from shame and feare,
Of such as seeke my soule to spill,
    Let not their counsell (Lord) preuaile,
    To force my hart to yeeld or quaile.

How frames it with your sober lookes,
To shroud such bent of lewd conceites?
What hope hath pla'st me in your bookes,
That files me fit, for such deceites?
    I hope that time hath made you see,
No cause that breeds these thoughts in mee.

Your feruent loue is filthy lust,
And therefore leaue to talke of loue,
Your truth is treason vnder trust,
A Kite in shape of hurtlesse Doue,
    You offer more then friendship wold,
    To giue vs brasse in steed of gold.

Such secret friends to open foes,
Do often change with euery wind,
Such wandring fits, where follie groes,
Are certaine signes of wauering mind,
 A fawning face, and faithlesse hart,
 In secret loue, breeds open smart.

No sinne to breake the wedlocke faith?
No sinne to swim in Sodomes sinke?
O sinne the seed and sting of death!
O sinnefull wretch that so doth thinke!
 Your grauest men with all their schooles,
 That taught you thus, were heathē fooles./ [23b

Your lewd examples will not serue,
To frame a vertue from a vice,
When *Dauid* and his Sonne did swerue,
From lawfull rule, though both were wise,
 Yet both were plagu'd, as you may see,
 With mightie plagues of each degree.

CANT. XXVII.

D. B. A French man.

FRom whence proceeds this sodaine change?
From whence this quainte and coye speech?
  Where did you learne to looke so strange?
What Doctor taught you thus to preach?
    Into my hart it can not sinke,
    That you doe speake, as you doe thinke.

Your smiling face, and glauncing eye,
(That promise grace, and not despite)
With these your words doe not agree,
That seeme to shun your chiefe delight,
    But giue me leaue, I thinke it still,
    Your words doe wander from your will,

Of women now the greatest part,
Whose place and age doe so require,
Do chuse a friend, whose faithfull hart,
May quench the flame of secret fire,
    Now if your liking be not pla'st,
    I know you will chuse one at last. /   [24*a*

F

Then chusing one, let me be he,
If so our hidden fancies frame,
Because you are the onely she,
That first inrag'd my fancies flame,
    If first you graunt me this good will,
    My hart is yours, and shall be still.

I haue a Farme that fell of late,
Woorth fortie pounds, at yearely rent,
That will I giue to mend your state,
And proue my loue is truely ment,
    Let not my sute be flat denide,
    And what you want, shall be supplide.

Our long acquaintance makes me bold;
To shew my greife, to ease my mind,
For new found friends, change not the old,
The like perhaps you shall not find,
    Be not too rash, take good aduice;
    Your hap is good, if you be wise.

CANT. XXVIII,

A V I S A.

MY hap is hard, and ouer bad,
To be misdeemd of euery man;
That thinke me quickly to be had,
That see me pleasant now and than:
  Yet would I not be much a greiu'd,
  If you alone were thus deceiu'd. /   [24b

But you alone are not deceiu'd,
With tising baytes of pleasant view,
But many others haue belieu'd,
And tride the same, as well as you,
  But they repent their folly past,
  And so will you, I hope at last.

You seeme, as though you lately came
From London, from some bawdie sell,
Where you haue met some wanton dame,
That knowes the trickes of whoores so well,
  Know you some wiues, vse more then one?
  Go backe to them, for here are none.

For here are none, that list to chuse,
A nouell chance, where old remaine,
My choice is past, and I refuse,
While this doth last, to chuse againe,
  While one doth liue, I will no more,
  Although I begge from dore to dore.

Bestow your farmes among your frinds,
Your fortie pounds can not prouoke,
The setled hart, whom vertue binds,
To trust the traines of hidden hooke,
  The labor's lost that you indure,
  To gorged Hauke, to cast the lure.

If lust had led me to the spoyle,
And wicked will, to wanton change,
Your betters that haue had the soyle,
Had caus'd me long ere this to range,
  But they haue left, for they did see,
  How far they were mistake of mee. / [H 2 5 *a*

CANT. XXIX.

D. B. A French man.

MIstake indeed, if this be true,
  If youth can yeeld to fauours foe;
If wisdome spring, where fancie grew;
But sure I thinke it is not so:
    Let faithfull meaning purchase trust,
    That likes for loue, and not for lust.

Although you sweare, you will not yeeld,
Although my death you should intend,
Yet will I not forsake the field,
But still remaine your constant frend,
    Say what you list, flie where you will,
    I am your thrall, to saue or spill.

You may command me out of sight,
As one that shall no fauour find,
But though my body take his flight,
Yet shall my hart remaine behind,
    That shall your guilty conscience tell,
    You haue not vs'd his master well.

His masters loue he shall repeate,
And watch his turne to purchase grace,
His secret eye shall lie in waite;
Where any other gaine the place:
    When we ech others can not see,
    My hart shall make you thinke of mee. / [25ᵇ

To force a fancie, where is none,
T'is but in vaine, it will not hold,
But where it growes it selfe alone,
A little fauour makes it bold,
    Till fancie frame your free consent,
    I must perforce, be needs content.

Though I depart with heauie cheare,
As hauing lost, or left my hart,
With one whose loue, I held too deare,
That now can smile, when others smart,
    Yet let your prisoner mercy see,
    Least you in time a prisoner bee.

CANT. XXX.

AVISA.

IT makes me smile to see the bent,
Of wandring minds with folly fed,
How fine they faine, how faire they paint,
To bring a louing soule to bed;
   They will be dead, except they haue,
   What so (forsooth) their fancie craue.

If you did seeke, as you pretend,
Not friendlesse lust, but friendly loue,
Your tongue and speeches would not lend,
Such lawlesse actions, so to moue,
   But you can wake, although you winke,
   And sweare the thing, you neuer thinke./[26a

To wauering men that speake so faire,
Let women neuer credit giue,
Although they weepe, although they sware,
Such fained shewes, let none belieue;
   For they that thinke their words be true.
   Shall soone their hastie credit rue.

Catullus.
Tum iam
nulla viro
iuranti
fœmina
credat.
Nulla viri
speret,ser-
monesesse
fideles.

Qui dum aliquid cupiens animus prægestit apisci, Nil metuunt iurare, nihil promittere parcunt.

Sed simul æc cupidæ mentis satiata libido est, Dicta nihil metuere, nihil periuria curant.

Combat betweene reasō and appetite. No constant loue where vnconstant affections rule. That loue only constant that is grounded on vertue.

When ventring lust doth make them dare,
The simple wenches to betray,
For present time they take no care,
What they doe sweare, nor what they say,
　　But hauing once obtaind the lot,
　　Their words and othes are all forgot.

Let rouing Prince from Troyes sacke,
Whose fauning fram'd Queen *Dido's* fall,
Teach women wit, that wisdome lacke,
Mistrust the most, beware of all,
　　When selfewill rules, where reason sate,
　　Fond women oft repent too late.

The wandring passions of the mind;
Where constant vertue bares no sway,
Such franticke fickle chaunges find,
That reason knowes not where to stay,
　　How boast you then of constant loue,
　　Where lust all vertue doth remoue? /　　[26b

T. B. Being somewhat grieued *with this aunswere, after long* absence and silence, at length writeth, as followeth.

CANT. XXXI,

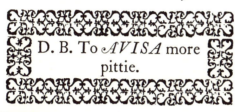

D. B. To *AVISA* more
pittie.

Here is a cole that burnes the more,
The more ye cast colde water neare,
Like humor feedes my secret sore,
Not quencht, but fed by cold dispaire,
The more I feele, that you disdaine,
The faster doth my loue remaine.

In grace they find a burning soile,
That fumes in nature like the same,
Colde water makes the hotter broyle,
The greater frost, the greater flame,
So frames it with my loue or lost,
That fiercely fries amidst the frost.

Canol cole found in many places of England. *Nympaus locus Leonicus de varia Histor.*fol. '98. By the Ionian Sea there is a place that burnes continually, and the more water is cast into it, the more it flames.

My hart inflam'd with quenchlesse heate,
Doth fretting fume in secret fire,
These hellish torments are the meate,
That dayly feede this vaine desire;
  Thus shall I grone in gastly griefe,
  Till you by mercy send reliefe. | [27a

You first inflam'd my brimstone thought,
Your faining fauour witcht mine eye,
O lucklesse eye, that thus hast brought,
Thy masters hart to striue awrye,
  Now blame your selfe, if I offend,
  The hurt you made, you must amend.

With these my lines I sent a Ring,
Least you might thinke you were forgot,
The posie meanes a pretie thing,
That bids you, Do but dally not,
  Do so sweete hart, and doe not stay,
  For daungers grow from sound delay.

Fiue winters Frosts haue say'd to quell
These flaming fits of firme desire,
Fiue Sommers sunnes can not expell
The cold dispaire, that feeds the fire,
  This time I hope, my truth doth trie,
  Now yeeld in time, or else I die.

                    Dudum beatus,
                    D. B.

CANT. XXXII.

A V I S A. To D. B. more
wisdome and feare of God.

/[27*b*]

T*He Indian men haue found a plant,*
  Whose vertue, mad conceits doth quell,
This roote (me thinks) you greatly want,
This raging madnes to repell,
    If rebell fancie worke this spite,
    Request of God a better sprite.

If you by folly did offend,
By giuing raines vnto your lust,
Let wisdome now these fancies end,
Sith thus vntwin'd is all your trust,
    If wit to will, willneeds resigne,
    Why should your fault be counted mine?

Your Ring and letter that you sent,
I both returne from whence they came,
As one that knowes not what is ment,
To send or write to me the same,
    You had your aunswere long before,
    So that you need to send no more.

The roote
Baaras is
good to
deliuer
them that
are
possessed
with euill
sprites.
Iosephus.

Your chosen posie seemes to show,
That all my deeds but dallings bee,
I neuer dallyed that I know,
And that I thinke, you partly see,
    I shewde you first my meaning plaine,
    The same is yet, and shall remaine.

Time pur-
geth
cholericke
humors,
and the
bloud

Some say that Tyme *doth purge the blood,*
And franticke humors brings to frame,
I maruaile time hath done no good,
Your long hid griefes and qualmes to tame?
    What secret hope doth yet remaine,
    That makes these sutes reuiue againe? / [28a

But did you will, and that in hast,
Except you find some quicke reliefe,
I'le warrant you, your life at last,
While foolish loue is all your griefe,
    As first I said, so say I still,
    I can not yeeld, nor euer will.

Alwaies the same,
Auisa.

CANT XXXIII.

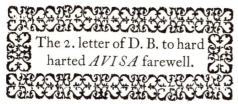

The 2. letter of D. B. to hard
harted *AVISA* farewell.

Find it true, that some haue said,
It's hard to loue, and to be wise,
For wit is oft by loue betraid,
And brought a sleepe, by fond deuise,
  Sith faith no fauour can procure,
  My patience must, my paine indure.

Difficile
est
diligere,
& Sapere.
Vulteius.

When womens wits haue drawne the plot,
And of their fancie laid the frame,
Then that they holde, where good or not,
No force can moue them from the same:
  So you, because you first denide,
  Do thinke it shame, for that to slide. |

[31 *b*

*Non si
fœminium
crebro ca-
put igne
refūdas,
Ingenii
mutes
primæ me-
talla sui.*

As faithfull friendship mou'd my tongue,
Your secret loue, and fauour craue;
And as I neuer did you wrong,
This last request so let me haue;
  Let no man know what I did moue,
  Let no man know, that I did loue;

That I will say, this is the worst,
When this is said, then all is past,
Thou proud *Auisa*, were the first,
Thou hard *Auisa*, art the last,
 Though thou in sorrow make me dwell,
 Yet loue will make me wish thee well.

Write not againe, except you write,
This onely gentle word, I will,
This onely word will bring delite,
The rest will breede but sorrow still,
 God graunt you gaine that you desire,
 By keeping that, which I require.

Yet will I listen now and then,
To see the end, my mind will craue,
Where you will yeeld to other men,
The thing that I could neuer haue.
 But what to me? where false or true,
 Where liue or die, for aye Adue.

Fortuna ferenda.

D. B. / [132a

DYDIMVS HARCO.
A NG L O-GE R-
MANVS.

CANT. XXXIIII.

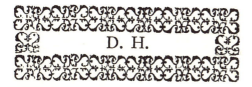

D. H.

 Haue to say, yet can not speake,
The thing that I would gladly say,
My hart is strong, though tong be weake,
Yet will I speake it, as I may.
 And if I speake not as I ought,
 Blame but the error of my thought,

And if I thinke not as I should,
Blame loue that bad me so to thinke;
And if I say not what I would,
T'is modest shame, that makes me shrinke,
 For sure their loue is very small,
 That can at first expresse it all.

Forgiue my blush, if I doe blush,
You are the first I euer tride,
And last whose conscience I will crush,
If now at first I be denide,
  I must be plaine then giue me leaue,
  I can not flatter nor deceiue. /   [32b

You know that Marchaunts ride for gaine,
As chiefe foundations of their state,
You see that we refuse no paine,
To rise betime, and trauell late,
  But farre from home, this is the spite,
  We want some times our chiefe delite.

I am no Saint, I must confesse,
But naturde like to other men,
My meaning you may quickly guesse,
I loue a woman now and then,
  And yet it is my common vse,
  To take aduise, before I chuse.

I oft haue seene the Western part,
And therein many a pretie elfe,
But found not any in my hart,
I like so well as of your selfe;
  And if you like no worse of mee,
  We may perhaps in time agree.

CANT XXXV.

A V I S A.

WHen first you did request to talke
  With me alone a little space,
When first I did consent to walke
With you alone within this place,
    From this your sage, and sober cheare,
    I thought some graue aduise to heare. / [33 *a*

Some say that womens faces faine
A modest shew, from wanton hart;
But giue me leaue, I see it plaine,
That men can play a duble part,
    I could not dreame, that I should find
    In lustlesse shew, such lustfull mind.

You make as though you would not speake,
As vnacquainted yet with loue,
As though your mind you could not breake,
Nor how these secret matters moue,
    You blush to speake, Alas the blush,
    Yet this is all not worth a rush.

G

Such slie conceites are out of ioynt,
So foule within, so faire without,
Not worth in proofe a threden poynt:
But now to put you out of doubt,
    Your thought is far deceiu'd of mee,
    As you in time shall plainely see.

If you had knowne my former life,
With spotlesse fame that I haue held,
How first a maide, and then a wife,
These youthly sutes I haue repeld,
    You would (I hope) correct your rate,
    That iudge me thus a common mate.

Whome you haue seene, I doe not care,
Nor reck not what you did request,
I am content this flout to beare,
In that you say, you like me best,
    And if you wish that you agree,
    Correct your wrong conceite of mee. / [33*b*

CANT. XXXVI.

D. H.

THe lymed bird, by foulers traine,
 Intrapt by view of pleasant baite,
Would faine vnwind himselfe againe;
But feeles too late the hid desaite:
  So I haue found the clasping lyme,
  That will sticke fast for longer tyme.

There is a floud, whose riuers runne,
Like streames of Milke, and seemes at first,
Extreamely colde, all heate to shunne,
But stay a while, and quench your thirst,
  Such vehement heate there will arise,
  As greater heate none may deuise.

These strange effects I find inrold,
Within this place, since my returne,
My first affections were but cold,
But now I feele them fiercely burne,
  The more you make such strange retire,
  The more you draw my new desire.

In Italy is a certaine water that falleth into the Riuer Anion, of colour white, and at first seemes to bee wonderfull colde, but being a while in it, it heateth the body more extreamely. *Leonicus de varia Histor.*

You thinke perchance I doe but iest,
Or I your secrets will bewray,
Or hauing got that I request,
With false *Aeneas* steale away,
    If you suspect that I will range,
    Let God forsake me, when I change. / [34*a*

I will not bost me of my wealth,
You shall no Gold nor Iewels want,
You see I am in perfect health,
And if you list to giue your grant,
    A hundreth pounds shall be your hire,
    But onely doe that I require.

And here's a Bracelet to begin,
Worth twentie Angels to be sold,
Besides the rest, this shall you win,
And other things not to be told,
    And I will come but now and then,
    To void suspect, none shall know when.

CANT. XXXVII.

WHy then your cõscience doth declare
  A guilty mind that shunnes the light,
A spotlesse conscience need not feare,
The tongues of men, nor yet the sight,
    Your secret slides doe passe my skill,
    And plainely shewe your workes are ill.

Your words command the lawlesse rite,
Of *Platoes* lawes that freedome gaue,
That men and women for delight,
Might both in common freely haue,
    Yet God doth threaten cruell death,
    To them that breake their wedlocke faith./[34b

The Bee beares honie in her mouth,
Yet poysoned sting in hinder part,
The spring is sweete where pleasure growth,
The fall of leafe brings storming smart,
    Vaine pleasure seemes most sweete at first,
    And yet their end is still accurst.

In Plato his common wealth all women were common, contrary to the commandement of God. Exod. 20, 14. Leuit 18. 20. 29.

Strange pleasure seemes sweete at the beginning, but their end is as bitter wormewood Prouer. 5. 3. 4. Prouer. 6. 27.

Non tanti emam pœnitere, Filthy heathen lawes. In Cyprus, their may-dens be-fore the time of their mariage were set open to euery man to gaine their dow-rie. Iusti-ne.

The Babilo-nians had a cus-tome, that if any were poore, they should procure their daughters and wiues to get mony with their bodies. Herodot. *Formosœ, pretio capiuntur auarœ. Imitantur hamos Dona. Fœmina prostituit seseque Munera donat. Feminœ se vendit quœ data dona capit, Vulteius.*

What bosome beares hote burning coles,
And yet consumes not with the same?
What feete tread fire with bared soles,
And are not synged with the flame?
    Then stay my friend, make no such hast,
    To buy *Repentaunce* at the last.

I am not of the Cyprian sort,
Nor yet haue learnd the common vse
Of Bable dames, in filthy sport,
For gaine no commers to refuse,
    What stormes or troubles euer grow,
    I list not seeke my liuing so.

Your gorgious gifts, your golden hookes,
Doe moue but fooles to looke aside,
The wise will shunne such craftie crookes,
That haue such false resemblance tride:
    But men are sure, that they will lift,
    That are content to take a gift. /   [35*a*

CANT. XXXVIII.

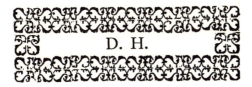

D. H.

NAy then farewell, if this be so,
  If you be of the purer stampe,
Gainst wind and tide I can not roe,
I haue no oyle to feede that lampe,
    Be not too rash, denie not flat,
    For you refuse, you know not what.

But rather take a farther day,
For farther triall of my faith,
And rather make some wise delay,
To see and take some farther breath:
    He may too rashly be denide,
    Whose faithfull hart was neuer tride.

And though I be by Iury cast,
Yet let me liue a while in hope,
And though I be condemnde at last,
Yet let my fancie haue some scope,
    And though the body flie away,
    Yet let me with the shadow play.

Will you receiue, if I doe send
A token of my secret loue?
And stay vntill you see the end
Of these effects, that fancie moue?
   Grant this, and this shall salue my sore,
   Although you neuer grant me more. / [35b

And thus at first let this suffise,
Inquire of me, and take the vewe
Of myne estate, with good aduise,
And I will do the like by you;
   And as you like, so frame your loue,
   But passe no promise till you proue.

This haue I said to shew my bent,
But no way spoken to offend,
And though my loue cannot relent,
Yet passed errors will I mend,
   Keepe close the Tenor of our talke,
   And say, we did for pleasure walke.

CANT XXXIX.

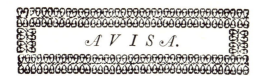

THen iugling mates do most deceaue,
  And most delude the dazeled sight,
When vp they turne their folded sleeue,
With bared armes to woorke their slight,
  When sharpe-set Foxe begins to preach,
  Let goslings keepe without his reach.

And will you haue me set a day,
To feede your hope with vaine delayes?
Well, I will doo as you do say,
And posse you vp with fainting stayes,
  That day shall breake my plighted faith,
  That drawes my last and gasping breath./ [K 36 *a*

If you will hope, then hope in this,
Ile neuer grant that you require:
If this you hope, you shall not misse,
But shall obtaine your hopes desire,
  If other hope you do retaine,
  Your labor's lost, your hope is vaine.

The child that playes with sharpned tooles,
Doth hurt himselfe for want of wit,
And they may well be counted fooles,
That wrastle neere a dangerous pit:
　　Your loose desire doth hope for that,
　　Which I must needes deny you flat.

Send mee no tokens of your lust,
Such giftes I list not to receiue,
Such guiles shall neuer make me trust,
Such broad-layde baytes cannot deceiue,
　　For they to yeeld do then prepare,
　　That grant to take such proffred ware.

The wo-
man that
receiueth
giftes of
such
sutors,
selleth
her selfe
& her
liberty.

If this be it you haue to say,
You know my mynd which cannot change,
I must be gon, I cannot stay,
No fond delight can make me range,
　　And for a farewell, this I sweare,
　　You get not that I hold so deare. /　[36*b*

After long absence, D H. happening to come *in on a tyme sodenly to her house, and finding her* all alone amongst her maides that were spinning, sayd *nothing, but going home wrate these verses following,* which he called his Dum habui. and sent them vnto her.

CANT. XL.

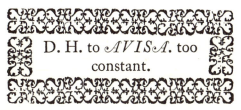

D. H. to *AVISA*. too constant.

Hyl'st erst I had my libertie,
To range the woodes where fancy list,
The cause of all my miserie,
By heedlesse hast my way I mist,
Vntill I found within a plaine,
A Christall Well, where Nimphes remaine.

As weary of this wild-goose race,
That led askance, I know not where,
I chose at length a shadow place,
To take the cold and pleasant ayre,
  But from the brinke of that same well,
  I saw my heauen, or els my hell.

I saw a byrde from ioyning groue,
That soaring came with comely grace,
The Lillie and Vermillion stroue,
In mayden-like and louely face,
    With seemely armes instead of winges,
    No clawes, but fingers set with ringes. | [37a

And in her hand she held a dart,
As being of Diana's trayne,
O that's the cause of all my smart,
And breeder of this endlesse paine,
    The thing I sought not, there I find,
    And lost the freedome of my mind.

While on her eies, my eies did hang,
From rolling eie there sprange a glance,
And therewith heard a sodayne clang,
That strake me in a deadly trance.
    But wak't I sawe blind Cupids craft,
    And in my hart the golden shaft.

I sewd for grace, but she deny'd.
Her laughty lookes she cast awry,
And when my folly she espy'd,
She laught to see my misery:
    Away she soares, and from my sight
    She smiling takes her parting flight.

You are the byrde that bred the bane,
That swelleth thus in restlesse thought,
You are the snare that thus haue tane,
And sences all to thraldome brought,
   You are the Iaylor that do keepe,
   Your frend in bandes, and dungeon deepe.

Renowmed chaste Penelope,
With all her wordes could not redryue
Her sutors, still she set a day,
In which she would them answere giue,
   When threedy spindle full was grow'n,
   Then would she chuse one for her ow'n. / [37b

They dayly came to see the end,
And euery man doth hope to bee
The chosen man, to be her frend,
But womens wyles here men may see,
   Her Spill was neuer fully spone,
   For night vndid that day had done.

I hope the like you haue decreed,
That found you spinning but of late,
Would God your Spill were full of threed,
That might releeue my wretched state,
   I will forget the wronges are past,
   So you will chuse me at the last.

Chuse one at length, I know you will,
Let tryed faith for ten yeares space,
How euer that your spindle fill,
With ioy possesse that emptie place,
   And if you will, I do protest,
   My loue shall far surmount the rest.

These lines that hope for better speed,
As louing spyes are sent to see,
Where you haue sponne vp all your threed,
And what good hap is left for mee:
   Let there returne, yet make him glad,
   Whome loues dispayre hath made so sad.

D. H. / [38a

CANT. XLI.

Auisa her answere to D. H.
a finall resolution.

F I be of Diana's *trayne,*
As trewe it is I must confesse,
I meruaile that you striue in vayne,
Where frutelesse hope yeelds no redresse:
   For they must needes continue sad
That seeke for that, will not be had.

What seruile follie doth possesse
Your base conceite, that can abyde
Such piteous plaintes, and sutes addresse,
To them that do your sutes deryde?
    For I can hardly thinke them wyse,
    That try againe, repulsed thryse.

No Hellens rape, nor Troian warre,
My louing mate hath fors't away,
No Iunoes wrath, to wander farre,
From louing bed can make him stray,
    Nor stay at all in forraine land,
    But here I haue him still at hand. / [38b

My sweet Vlisses *neuer stayes*
From his desyred home so long,
That I should need such rare delayes
To Shield me from intended wrong,
    My chiefe delightes are alwayes nye,
    And in my bosome sweetely lye.

The Spindle that you see me driue,
Hath fyld the spill so often trend,
My hart is fixt, since I did giue
My wedlocke faith to chosen frend,
    Then leaue to sewe, since that you see
    Your hap debarres your hope from mee.

I vse not oft to make reply
To lines that yeelde such wanton store,
Let this suffice, that I deny,
And after this, looke for no more,
   My choise is bound, by lawfull band,
   My oath is past, and that shall stand.

Alway the same
Auisa. | [39a

CANT. XLII.

D. H. to chast *Auisa* per-
petuall constancy.

His is inough: now I haue done,
I thinke indeed you do not faine,
As others haue, that haue beene wonne
In shorter space, with lesser paine,
And sith you will not yeeld in deed
To these my wordes, yet take good heed.

My former loue was onely lust,
As you in deed did truly say,
And they, such loue that rashly trust,
Do plant the plot of swift decay:
> *But they whom Grace doth make so wise,*
> *To high renowne, will surely ryse.*

If you had had a waxye hart,
That would haue melt at hot desyre,
Or chaffye thoughtes that could haue start,
And yeeld to burne at euery fyre,
> *What ere I did, or sayd before,*
> *I should haue thought you but a whore.*

Though saylers loue the common Port,
As safest harbour where to rest,
Yet wise men seeke the strongest fort,
And paper castells most detest:
> *Men cannot loue such as they know,*
> *Will yeeld at sight of euery blow.* | [39b

But now my loue by vertue bound,
No stormie blastes can make it quaile,
Your constant mind a frend hath found,
Whose honest loue shall neuer faile,
> *A faithfull frend in honest loue,*
> *Whom lewd affections shall not moue.*

O violata,
vale, vale
ó violata,
placebas,
Inuiolata
noces nunc
violata
mihi,
Vulteius.

Sic virgo
dum in-
tacta
manet, tū
chara suis,
sed cum
amisit
polluto
corpore
florem.
Nec pueris
iucunda
manet, nec
chara pu-
ellis.
Catullus.

H

If you this wanton fault forgiue,
No time in me shall euer find
Such lewd attemptes, while I do liue,
Now that I know your constant mynd,
   My pen doth write, my hart hath swore,
   My tounge such speech shall vse no more.

A thousand tymes I loue no more,
Then if I had my purpose wonne,
Of common loue I make no store,
But leaue it there where I begunne,
   What oddes there is, now you may proue,
   Twixt wicked lust and honest loue.

Now grant I pray this last request,
That fraudlesse hart doth frendly send,
That if my fayth deserue it best,
Accept me for your honest frend:
   And if I seeke your spoile, or shame,
   Then raze me out, and blot my name.

And if I shall this fauour find,
Then weare this ring, though you be loth,
As token of my simple mynd,
And perfect band of faithfull oath:
   The posye is, No frend to faith
   That will remaine, till both our death./[L 40 *a*

Esteeme not this a painted bait,
Or golden ball cast to deceaue:
If I do meane such lewd desait,
Let God my soule in tormentes leaue:
  I say no more, but thus I end,
  In honest loue your faithful frend.

D. H.

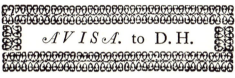

AVISA. to D. H.

CANT, XLIII.

Y Ou know that I haue laid my rest,
  From which my mind shall neuer swerue,
If all be true that you protest,
Then shall you find, as you deserue:
  All hidden truth tyme will bewraie,
  This is as much as I can saie.

Alway the same
Auisa.

CANT. XLIIII.

Henrico Willobego. Italo-Hispalensis.

H. W. being sodenly infected with the con-
tagion of a fantasticall fit, at the first sight of *A,*

pyneth a while in secret griefe, at length not able any longer to indure the burning heate of so feruent a humour, bewrayeth the secresy of his disease vnto his familiar frend W. S. who not long before had tryed the cur- / tesy of the like [40*b* passion, and was now newly recouered of the like infection; yet finding his frend let bloud in the same vaine, he took pleasure for a tyme to see him bleed, & in steed of stopping the issue, he inlargeth the wound, with the sharpe rasor of a willing conceit, perswading him that he thought it a matter very easy to be compassed, & no doubt with payne, diligence & some cost in time to be obtayned. Thus this miserable comforter comforting his frend with an impossibilitie, eyther for that he now would secretly laugh at his frends folly, that had giuen occasion not long before vnto others to laugh at his owne, or because he would see whether an other could play his part better then himselfe, & in vewing a far off the course of this louing Comedy, he determined to see whether it would sort to a happier end for this new actor, then it did for the old player. But at length this Comedy was like to haue growen to a Tragedy, by the weake & feeble estate that H. W. was brought vnto, by a desperate vewe of an impossibility of obtaining his purpose, til Time &

Necessity, being his best Phisitions brought him
a plaster, if not to heale, yet in part to ease his
maladye. In all which discourse is liuely represented the vnrewly rage of vnbrydeled fancy, hauing
the raines to roue at liberty, with the dyuers &
sundry changes of affections & temptations,
which Will, set loose from Reason, can deuise. &c.
/ [41 *a*

H. W.

Hat sodaine chance or change is this,
That doth bereaue my quyet rest?
What surly cloud eclipst my blisse,
What sprite doth rage within my brest?
    Such fainty qualmes I neuer found,
    Till first I saw this westerne ground.

Can change of ayre complexions change,
And strike the senses out of frame?
Though this be true, yet this is strange,
Sith I so lately hither came:
    And yet in body cannot find
    So great a change as in my mynd.

My lustlesse limmes do pyne away,
Because my hart is dead within,
All liuely heat I feele decay,
And deadly cold his roome doth win,
    My humors all are out of frame,
    I frize amid'st the burning flame.

I haue the feauer Ethicke right,
I burne within, consume without,
And hauing melted all my might,
Then followes death, without all doubt:
    O fearefull foole, that know my greefe,
    Yet sew and seeke for no releefe. /   [41*b*

I know the tyme, I know the place,
Both when and where my eye did vew
That nouell shape, that frendly face,
That so doth make my hart to rew,
    O happy tyme if she inclyne,
    If not, O wourth theese lucklesse eyne.

I loue the seat where she did sit,
I kisse the grasse, where she did tread,
Me thinkes I see that face as yet,
And eye, that all these turmoyles breed,
    I enuie that this seat, this ground,
    Such frendly grace and fauour found.

I dream't of late, God grant that dreame
Protend my good, that she did meete
Me in this greene by yonder streame,
And smyling did me frendly greete:
   Where wandring dreames be iust or
   I mind to try ere it be long.   (wrong,

But yonder comes my faythfull frend,
That like assaultes hath often tryde,
On his aduise I will depend,
Where I shall winne, or be denyde,
   And looke what counsell he shall giue,
   That will I do, where dye or liue. /   [42a

CANT. XLV.

W. S.

WEll met, frend Harry, what's the cause
   You looke so pale with Lented
Your wanny face & sharpened nose (cheeks?
Shew plaine, your mind some thing mislikes,
   If you will tell me what it is,
   Ile helpe to mend what is amisse.

What is she, man, that workes thy woe,
And thus thy tickling fancy moue?
Thy drousie eyes, & sighes do shoe,
This new disease proceedes of loue,
 Tell what she is that witch't thee so,
 I sweare it shall no farder go.

A heauy burden wearieth one,
Which being parted then in twaine,
Seemes very light, or rather none,
And boren well with little paine:
 The smothered flame, too closely pent,
 Burnes more extreame for want of vent.

So sorrowes shrynde in secret brest,
Attainte the hart with hotter rage,
Then griefes that are to frendes exprest,
Whose comfort may some part asswage:
 If I a frend, whose faith is tryde,
 Let this request not be denyde. / [42b

Excessiue griefes good counsells want,
And cloud the sence from sharpe conceits;
No reason rules, where sorrowes plant,
And folly feedes, where fury fretes,
 Tell what she is, and you shall see,
 What hope and help shall come from mee.

CANT. XLVI.

H. W.

Seest yonder howse, where hanges the badge
Of Englands Saint, when captaines cry
  Victorious land, to conquering rage,
Loe, there my hopelesse helpe doth ly:
  And there that frendly foe doth dwell,
  That makes my hart thus rage and swell,

CANT. XLVII.

W. S.

Well, say no more: I know thy griefe,
  And face from whence these flames
It is not hard to fynd reliefe,   (aryse,
If thou wilt follow good aduyse:
  She is no Saynt, She is no Nonne,
  I thinke in tyme she may be wonne: /   [43*a*

*Arsvetera-
toria.*

At first repulse you must not faint,
Nor flye the field though she deny
You twise or thrise, yet manly bent,
Againe you must, and still reply:
　　When tyme permits you not to talke,
　　Then let your pen and fingers walke.

Apply her still with dyuers thinges,

*Munera
(crede
mihi) pla-
cant homi-
nesq;
Deosq;.*

(For giftes the wysest will deceaue)
Sometymes with gold, sometymes with
No tyme nor fit occasion leaue,　　(ringes,
　　Though coy at first she seeme and wielde,
　　These toyes in tyme will make her yielde.

Looke what she likes; that you must loue,
And what she hates, you must detest,
Where good or bad, you must approue,
The wordes and workes that please her best:
　　If she be godly, you must sweare,
　　That to offend you stand in feare.

Wicked
wiles to
deceaue
witles wo-
men.

You must commend her louing face,
For women ioy in beauties praise,
You must admire her sober grace,
Her wisdome and her vertuous wayes,
　　Say, t'was her wit & modest shoe,
　　That made you like and loue her so.

You must be secret, constant, free,
Your silent sighes & trickling teares,
Let her in secret often see,
Then wring her hand, as one that feares
    To speake, then wish she were your wife,
    And last desire her saue your life. /   [43*b*]

When she doth laugh, you must be glad,
And watch occasions, tyme and place,
When she doth frowne, you must be sad,
Let sighes & sobbes request her grace:
    Sweare that your loue is truly ment,
    So she in tyme must needes relent.

C A N T. XLVIII.

H. W.

THe whole to sicke good counsell giue,
  Which they themselues cannot performe,
Your wordes do promise sweet reliefe,
To saue my ship from drowning storme:
    But hope is past, and health is spent,
    For why my mynd is *Mal-content.*

The flowring hearbes, the pleasant spring,
That deckes the fieldes with vernant hew,
The harmelesse birdes, thatsweetly sing,
My hidden griefes, do still renew:
　The ioyes that others long to see,
　Is it that most tormenteth mee.

To dis-
paire of
good suc-
cesse in
the begin-
ning of a-
ny action,
is always
a secret &
most cer-
taine
fore-warn-
ing of ill
successe,
that in-
deed doth
often fol-
low.

I greatly doubt, though March be past,
Where I shall see that wished May,
That can recure that balefull blast,
Whose cold dispaire wrought my decay:
　My hopelesse cloudes, that neuer cleere,
　Presage great sorrowes very neere./　[M 44 *a*

I mirth did once, and musicke loue,
Which both as now, I greatly hate:
What vncouth sprite my hart doth moue,
To loath the thing, I lou'd so late?
　My greatest ease in deepest mone,
　Is when I walke my selfe alone.

Where thinking on my hopelesse hap,
My trickling teares, like riuers flow,
Yet fancy lulles me in her lap,
And telles me, lyfe from death shall grow:
　Thus flattering hope makes me belieue;
　My griefe in tyme shall feele relieue.

Good fortune helpes the ventering wight,
That hard attempts dare vndertake:
But they that shun the doubtful fight,
As coward drudges, doth forsake:
  Come what there will, I meane to try,
  Wher winne, or lose, I can but dye.

Audaces
fortuna
iuuat,
timidosq;
repellit.

CANT. XLIX.

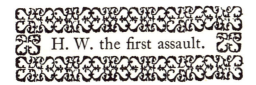

H. W. the first assault.

Pardon (sweet wench) my fancies fault,
  If I offend to shew my smart,
    Your face hath made such fierce assault,
And battred so my fencelesse hart:
  That of my foe, my lyfe to saue,
  For grace I am constraind to craue. /   [44ᵇ

The raging Lyon neuer rendes
The yeelding pray, that prostrate lyes,
No valiant captayne euer bendes
His force against surrendering cryes:
Here I surrender roome and right,
And yeeld the fort at captaines sight.

You are the chieftaine, that haue layd
This heauie siege to strengthlesse fort,
And fancy that my will betrayd,
Hath lent dispaire his strongest port:
   Your glauncing eyes as Cannon shot,
   Haue pearst my hart, and freedome got.

When first I saw that frendly face,
Though neuer seene before that day,
That wit, that talke, that sober grace,
In secret hart thus did I say:
   God prosper this, for this is she,
   That ioy or woe must bring to me.

A thousand fewtures I haue seene,
For Trauelers change, & choyse shall see,
In Fraunce, in Flaunders, & in Spaine,
Yet none, nor none could conquere mee:
   Till now I sawe this face of thyne,
   That makes my wittes are none of myne.

I often said, yet there is one,
But where, or what I could not tell,
Whose sight my sence would ouercome,
I feard it still, I knew it well,
   And now I know you are the She,
   That was ordaind to vanquish me. /   [45a

CANT. L.

WHat song is this that you do sing,
   What tale is this that you do tell,
What newes is this that you do bring,
Or what you meane I know not well?
    If you will speake, pray speake it playne,
    Lest els perhaps you lose your payne.

My mynd surpris'd with houshold cares,
Tendes not darke riddles to vntwyne.
My state surcharg'd with great affares,
To Idle talke can lend no tyme;
    For if your speeches tend to loue,
    Your tonge in vaine such sutes will moue.

In greenest grasse the winding snake,
With poysoned sting is soonest found,
A cowardes tongue makes greatest cracke,
The emptiest caske yeeldes greatest sound,
    To hidden hurt, the bird to bring,
    The fouler doth most sweetly sing.

Idlenesse the mo-ther of all foolish wannesse.

Dauid be-
ing idle
fell to
strange
lust.
*Quæritur
Egistus,
quare fit
factus A-
dulter.*

If wandering rages haue possest
Your rouing mynd at randame bent;
If idle qualmes from too much rest,
Fond fancyes to your lust haue sent:
　　Cut off the cause that breedes your smart,
　　Then will your sicknesse soone depart./[45b

*In promp-
tu causa
est: De-
sidiosus
erat.*
Noble-
men gen-
tlemen,
and Cap-
taynes by
idlenesse
fall to all
kynd of
vices.

The restles mynd that reason wantes,
Is like the ship that lackes a sterne,
The hart beset with follyes plantes,
At wisdomes lore repynes to learne:
　　Some seeke and fynd what fancy list,
　　But after wish that they had mist.

Who loues to tread vnknowen pathes,
Doth often wander from his way,
Who longes to laue in brauest bathes,
Doth wash by night, and wast by day:
　　Take heed betyme, beware the pryse
　　Of wicked lust, if you be wyse.

CANT. LI.

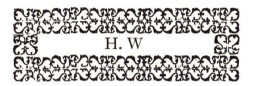

H. W

Vnwonted lyking breedes my loue,
   And loue the welspring of my griefe,
   This fancy fixt none can remoue,
None send redresse, none giue reliefe,
    But onely you, whose onely sight
    Hath fors't me to this pyning plight.

Loue oft doth spring from due desart,
As louing cause of true effect,
But myne proceeds from wounded hart,
As scholler to a nouell sect:
    I bare that lyking, few haue bore,
    I loue, that neuer lou'd before. /   [46 *a*

I loue, though doubtfull of successe,
As blindmen grope to try the way;
Yet still I loue because I gesse,
You loue, for loue cannot denay,
    Except you spring of sauadge kynd,
    Whome no desartes, nor loue can bynd.

I

Of all the graces that excell,
And vertues that are cheefly best,
A constant loue doth beare the bell,
And makes his owner euer blest:
    How blame you then the faithfull loue,
    That hath his praise from God aboue.

Can you withstand what fates ordayne?
Can you reproue dame Natures frame?
Where natures ioyne, shall will disclaime?
Acquite my loue, beare they the blame,
    That snuffe at faith, & looke so coy,
    And count true loue but for a toy.

If fortune say it shal be so,
Then though you lyke, yet shall you yeeld,
Say what you list, you cannot go
Vnconquerd thus from Cupids field,
    That loue that none could euer haue,
    I giue to you, and yours I craue, / [46*b*

CANT. LII

A V I S A.

WEll, you are bent I see, to try
The vtmost list of follies race,
Your fancy hath no power to fly
The luring baite of flattering grace,
  The fish that leapes & neuer lookes,
  Fyndes death vnwares in secret hookes.

You say you loue, yet shew no cause,
Of this your loue, or rather lust,
Or whence this new affection groes
Which though vntryde, yet we must trust,
  Dry reeds that quickly yeeld to burne,
  Soone out to flamelesse cinders turne.

Such raging loue in rangling mates,
Is quickly found, and sooner lost;
Such deepe deceate in all estates,
That spares no care, no payne nor cost:
  VVith flattering tongues, & golden giftes,
  To dryue poore women to their shiftes.

Examine well, & you shall see
Your truthlesse treason tearmed loue,
VVhat cause haue you to fancy mee,
That neuer yet had tyme to proue,
　　What I haue beene, nor what I am,
　　Where worthie loue, or rather shame?/[47ª

This loue that you to straungers bare,
Is like to headstrong horse and mule,
That ful-fed nyes on euery mare,
Whose lust outleapes the lawfull rule,
　　For here is seene your constant loue,
　　VVhome strange aspects so quickly moue.

Besides you know I am a wife,
Not free, but bound by plighted oath,
Can loue remaine, where filthy life
Hath staind the soile, where vertue gro'th?
　　Can loue indure, where faith is fled?
　　Can Roses spring, whose roote is dead?

True loue is constant in her choise,
But if I yeeld to chuse againe,
Then may you say with open voice,
This is her vse, this is her vaine,
　　She yeelds to all, how can you than
　　Loue her that yeeldes to euery man?

CANT. LIII.

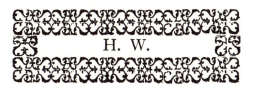

H. W.

IF feare and sorrow sharpe the wit,
  And tip the tongue with sweeter grace,
  Then will & style, must finely fit,
To paint my griefe, and waile my case:
    Sith my true loue is counted lust,
    And hope is rackt in spitefull dust. / [47*b*

The cause that made me loue so soone,
And feedes my mind with inward smart,
Springs not from Starres, nor yet the Moone,
But closly lies in secret hart:
    And if you aske, I can not tell,
    Nor why, nor how, this hap befell.

If birth or beautie could haue wrought,
In lustlesse hart this loues effect,
Some fairer farre my loue haue sought,
Whose louing lookes I did reiect.
    If now I yeeld without assault,
    Count this my fortune or my fault.

You are a wife, and you haue swore,
You will be true. Yet what of this?
Did neuer wife play false before,
Nor for her pleasure strike amis?
   Will you alone be constant still,
   When none are chast, nor euer will?

A man or woman first may chuse
The loue that they may after loth;
Wo can denie but such may vse
A second choice, to pleasure both?
   No fault to change the old for new;
   So to the second they be trew.

Your husband is a worthlesse thing,
That no way can content your mind,
That no way can that pleasure bring,
Your flowring yeares desire to find:
   This I will count my chiefest blisse,
   If I obtaine, that others misse. /   [N 48*a*

Ther's nothing gotten to be coye,
The purer stampe you must detest,
Now is your time of greatest ioye,
Then loue the friend that loues you best,
   This I will count my chiefest blisse,
   If I obtaine that others misse.

CANT. LIIII.

A V I S A.

THat others misse, you would obtaine,
    And want of this doth make you sad,
    I sorrow that you take such paine,
To seeke for that, will not be had,
    Your filed skill the power doth want,
    VVithin this plot such trees to plant.

Though some there be, that haue done ill,
And for their fancie broke their faith:
Yet doe not thinke that others will,
That feare of shame more then of death:
    A spotlesse name is more to me,
    Then wealth, then friends, then life can be.

Are all vnconstant, all vnsound?
VVill none performe their sworen vow?
Yet shall you say, that you haue found,
A chast, and constant wife I trow:
    And you shall see, when all is doone,
    VVhere all will yeeld, and all be woone./[48b

Though you haue bin at common schoole,
And enterd plaints in common place;
Yet you wil proue your selfe a foole,
To iudge all women void of grace:
    I doubt not but you will be brought,
    Soone to repent this wicked thought.

Your second change let them alow,
That list mislike their primer choice,
I lou'd him first, I loue him now,
To whom I gaue my yeelding voice,
    My faith and loue, I will not giue
    To mortall man, while he doth liue.

What loue is this, that bids me hate,
The man whom nature bids me loue?
What loue is this, that sets debate,
Twixt man and wife? but here I proue:
    Though smothed words seeme very kind,
    Yet all proceed from deuilish mind.

CANT. LV.

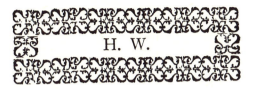

H. W.

FRom deuilish mind? well wanton well,
 You thinke your strength is very sure,
 You thinke all women to excell,
And all temptations to indure.
 These glorious braggs shew but your pride:
 For all will yeeld, if they be tride. / [49a

You are (I hope) as others bee,
A woman, made of flesh and blood,
Amongst them all, will you goe free,
When all are ill, will you be good?
 Assure your selfe, I do not faine,
 Requite my loue with loue againe

Let me be hangd if you be such,
As you pretend in outward shoe:
Yet I commend your wisdome much,
Which mou'd me first to loue you so:
 Where men no outward shewes detect,
 Suspicious minds can nil suspect.

But to the matter; tell me true,
Where you your fancie can incline,
To yeeld your loue, for which I sue,
As fortune hath intangled mine:
    For well I know, it's nothing good,
    To striue against the raging flood.

What you mislike, I will amend,
If yeares I want, why I will stay,
My goods and life here I will spend,
And helpe you still in what I may:
    For though I seeme a headlong youth,
    Let time be triall of my truth.

Your name by me shall not be crackt,
But let this tongue from out my iawes,
Be rent, and bones to peeces rackt,
If I your secrets doe disclose,
    Take good aduisement what you say,
    This is my good, or dismall day. / [49*b*

CANT. LVI.

A V I S A.

Y Es, so I will, you may be bold,
  Nor will I vse such strange delaies;
  But that you shall be quickly told,
How you shall frame your wandring waies:
  If you will follow mine aduise,
  Doubt not but you shall soone be wise.

To loue, excepting honest loue,
I can not yeeld, assure your mind;
Then leaue this frutelesse sute to moue,
Least like to *Sysyphus* you find,
  With endlesse labour, gainelesse paine,
  To role the stone that turnes againe.

You want no yeares, but rather wit,
And dew forecast in that you seeke,
To make your choice that best may fit,
And this is most that I mislieke;
  If you be free, liue where you list,
  But still beware of, Had I wist.

Serue God, and call to him for grace,
That he may stay your slipperie slides,
From treading out that sinfull trace,
That leades where endlesse sorrowe bides,
    Thus shall you wisely guide your feete;
    Though youth and wisedome seldome meete./[50a

And if you find, you haue no gift,
To liue a chast and mateless life,
Yet feare to vse vnlawfull shift,
But marry with some honest wife,
    With whom you may contented liue,
    And wandring mind from folly driue.

Fuggi quel pi-acer pre-sente, che ti da dolor futuro.

Fly present pleasure that doth bring
Insuing sorrow, paine and griefe;
Of death beware the poys'ned sting,
That hatcheth horror sance reliefe,
    Take this of me, and in the end
    I shall be thought your chiefest frend.

CANT. LVII.

H. W.

IF then the welspring of my ioy,
A floud of woe, in fine become,
If loue ingender loues annoy,
Then farewell life, my glasse is runne:
  If you thus constant still remaine;
  Then must I die, or liue in paine.

Thrice happie they, whose ioyned harts,
Vnited wils haue linckt in one,
Whose eies discerne the due desarts,
The griping griefe, and grieuous grone,
  That faith doth breed in setled mind,
  As fancies are by fates inclind. /   [50b

And shall I role the restlesse stone?
And must I proue the endlesse paine?
In curelesse care shall I alone,
Consume with griefe, that yeelds me gaine?
  If so I curse these eies of mine,
  That first beheld that face of thine.

Your will must with my woe dispence,
Your face the founder of my smart,
That pleasant looke fram'd this offence,
These thrilling gripes that gall my hart,
    Sith you this wound, and hurt did giue,
    You must consent to yeeld relieue.

How can I cease, while fancie guides
The restlesse raines of my desire?
Can reason rule, where folly bides?
Can wit inthrald to will retire?
    I little thought, I should haue mist,
    I neuer feard of, Had I wist.

Let old men pray, let setled heads
Inthrall their necks to wedlocke band,
Shrend golden gyues, who euer weds
With pleasant paine, shall take in hand:
    But I will be your faithful frend,
    If health by hope you yeeld to send. / [51 *a*

CANT. LVIII.

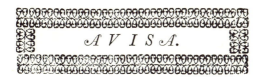

A V I S A.

WHat filthy folly, raging lust,
　　What beastly blindnes fancy breeds?
　　As though the Lord had not accurst,
With vengeance due, the sinfull deeds?
　Though vaine-led youth with pleasure swell,
　Yet marke these words that I shall tell.

Who so with filthy pleasure burnes;
His sinfull flesh with fierie flakes
Must be consum'd; whose soule returnes
To endlesse paine in burning lakes.
　You seeme by this, to wish me well,
　To teach me tread the path to hell.

*Gen.38.24
Whore-
moungers
burnt.*

Call you this (Loue) that bringeth sin,
And sowes the seeds of heauie cheere?
If this be loue, I pray begin,
To hate the thing I loue so deere;
　I loue no loue of such a rate,
　Nor fancie that, which God doth hate.

But what saith he that long had tryde

Prouer. 5.
3. Of harlots all the wanton slights;
Beware least that your hart betyde,
To fond affects by wanton sights:
    Their wandring eies, and wanton lookes
    Catch fooles as fish, with painted hookes./[51*b*

Their lippes with oyle and honie flow,
Their tongs are fraught with flattering guile;
Amidst these ioyes great sorrowes grow;
For pleasures flourish but a while,
    Their feete to death, their steps to hell,
    Do swiftly slide, that thus do mell.

Then flie this dead and dreadfull loue,
This signe of Gods reuenging ire;
Let loue of God such lust remoue,
And quench the flames of foule desire:
    If you will count me for your frend,
    You must both workes and words amend.

CANT LXI.

With this bitter reply of *Auisa*, H. W. being somewhat daunted, yet not altogether whithout hope, went home to his house, and there secretly in a melancolike passion wrote these verses following.

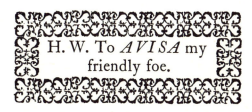

H. W. To *AVISA* my friendly foe.

THe busie Gnat about the candle, houering still *Sixaine,*
    doth flie,
The slimie Fish about the bayt, still wauering doth lie,
The fearefull Mouse about the trap doth often try his
    strength,
Vntill both Gnat, and Fish and Mouse, be taken at the
    length,
    Euen so vnhappie I, do like my greatest baine,
    Vnlesse you do with speede, release my mortall
    paine. |
                              [O 52 a

The light foote hart desires the waters brooke, *Qua-*
The dogge most sicke the greenest grasse doth craue. *traine.*

K

The wounded wight for surgeon still doth looke,
Vntill both hart, and dogge, and wight their medicine
haue:
   But I with griefe th'vnhappiest of them all,
   Do still delight to be my enemies thrall.

Deuxaine. *Mine enemie I say, though yet my sweetest frend,*
If of my sorrowes I may see some speedie holsome end.

F I N I S. Chi la dura, la Vince.

C A N T. LXII.

AVISA. her reply to H. VV.

T*He busie Gnat for want of wit,*
   Doth sindge his wings in burning flame,
   The Fish with baite will headlong flit,
Till she be choked with the same;
   So you with Gnat and Fish will play,
   Till flame and foode worke your decay.

The heedlesse Mouse, that tries the trap,
In hast to reach her harts desire,
Doth quickly find such quainte mishap,
That barres her strength from free retire,
   So you will neuer ceasse to craue,
   Till you haue lost that now you haue. | [52 b

The hart, the dogge, the wounded wight,
For water, grasse, and Surgeon call,
Their griefes and cures, are all but light,
But your conceite surpast them all;
  Except you change your wanton mind,
  You shall no ease, nor comfort find.

Alway the same
Auisa.

CANT. LXIII.

H.W. prosecuteth his sute.

Will not your laughty stomacke stoupe?
Will not this selfe conceite come downe?
As haggard louing mirthlesse coupe,
At friendly lure doth checke and frowne?
  Blame not in this the Faulkners skill,
  But blame the Hawkes vnbridled will.

Your sharp replies, your frowning cheare,
To absent lines, and present vew,
Doth aie redouble trembling feare,
And griping griefes do still renew,
  Your face to me my sole reliefe,
  My sight to you your onely griefe. /   [53 a

O lucklesse wretch, what hap had I,
To plant my loue in such a soile?
What furie makes me thus relie
On her that seekes my vtter spoile?
  O Gods of loue what signe is this,
  That in the first, I first should mis?

And can you thus increase my woe,
And will you thus prolong my paine?
Canst kill the hart that loues thee so,
Canst quit my loue with foule disdaine?
  And if thou canst, woe worth the place,
  Where first I saw that flattering face.

And shall my folly proue it trew,
That hastie pleasure doubleth paine,
Shall griefe rebound, where ioye grew?
Of faithfull hart is this the gaine?
  Me thinks for all your graue aduise,
  (Forgiue my thought) you are not wise.

Would God I could restraine my loue,
Sith you to loue me can not yeeld,
But I alas can not remoue
My fancie, though I die in feeld;
  My life doth on your loue depend,
  My loue and life at once must end.

CANT. LXIIII.

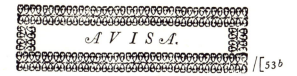

AVISA.

/[53^b]

W Hat witlesse errors do possesse
The wretched minds of louing fooles,
That breathlesse runne to such distresse,
That liuely heate fond sorrowe cooles?
   They reke not where they stand or fall,
   Deny them loue, take life and all.

It seemes a death to change their mind,
Or alter once their foolish will,
Such od conceites they seeke to find,
As may their childish fancies fill,
   It makes me smile thus, now and then,
   To see the guise of foolish men.

I can not stoupe to wandring lure;
My mind is one, and still the same;
While breath, while life, while daies indure,
I will not yeeld to worke my shame,
   Then if you striue and stirre in vaine,
   Blame but the fruites of idle braine.

If I do sometimes looke awrie,
As loth to see your blobered face,
And loth to heare a yong man crie,
Correct for shame this childish race,
    And though you weepe and waile to mee,
    Yet let not all these follies see.

Good *Harry* leaue these raging toyes,
That thus from restlesse fancie flow,
Vnfit for men, not meete for boyes,
And let's a while talke wisely now;
    If that you loue me as you say,
    Then cease such madnes to bewray. / [54 *a*

If honest loue could breed content,
And frame a liking to your will,
I would not sticke to giue consent,
To like you so, and loue you still,
    But while lust leades your loue awrie,
    Assure your selfe, I will denie.

CANT. LXV.

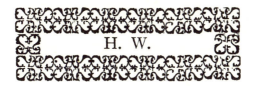

H. W.

ANd is it lust that welds my loue?
Or is it but your fond surmise?
Will you condemne, before you proue?
How can I thinke you to be wise?
    O faithfull hart, yet thrice accurst,
    That art misdeemd thus at the first.

If lust did rule my restlesse hart,
If onely lust did beare the sway,
I quickly could asswage my smart,
With choise, and change, for euery day,
    You should not laugh to see me weepe,
    If lust were it that strake so deepe.

And yet at first, before I knew,
What vaine it was that bled so sore,
Wher lust or loue, to proue it trew,
I tooke a salue that still before
    Was wont to helpe, I chose me one,
    With whom I quencht my lust alone./ [54^b

Yet this (sweete hart) could not suffise,
A bad
argument
to proue
good loue.
Nor any way content my mind,
I felt new qualmes, and new arise,
And stronger still, and strong I find,
    By this, I thus doe plainely proue,
    It is not lust, but faithfull loue.

And yet to proue my loue more sure,
And sith you will not false your faith,
This pining plight I will indure,
Till death do stop your husbands breath;
    To haue me then if you will say,
    I will not marrie, till that day.

If you will giue your full consent,
When God shall take your husbands life,
That then you will be well content,
To be my spouse and louing wife,
    I will be ioyfull as before,
    And till that time, will craue no more.

CANT, LXVI.

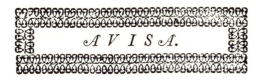

A V I S A.

NO more; no more, too much of this,
  And is mine ynch become an ell?
If thus you writh my words amis,
I must of force, bid you farwell,
   You shew in this your louing bent,
    To catch at that, I neuer ment. /   [55a

I thought at first, (but this my though
I must correct;) that simple loue,
In guilles hart these fits had wrought.
But I; too simple I, now proue,
   That vnder shew of great good will,
   My harts delight you seeke to spill.

He loues me well, that tils a trap,
Of deepe deceite, and deadly baine,
In dreadfull daungers thus to wrap
His friend by baites of flering traine:
   Though flattering tongues can paint it braue
   Your words do shew, what loue you haue.

I must consent, and you will stay
My husbands death. Obtaining this,
You thinke I could not say you Nay:
Nor of your other purpose mis,
   You are deceiu'd, and you shall trie,
   That I such faith, and friends defie.

Such fained, former, faithlesse plot
I most detest, and tell you plaine,
If now I were to cast my lot,
With free consent to chuse againe,
   Of all the men I euer knew,
   I would not make my choice of you.

Let this suffice, and do not stay
On hope of that which will not be,
Then cease your sute, go where you may,
Vaine is your trust, to hope on me.
   My choice is past, my hart is bent,
   While that remaines to be content. / [55*b*

Now hauing tract the winding trace
Of false resemblance, giue me leaue,
From this to shew a stranger grace,
Then heretofore, you did perceaue,
   Gainst frendlesse loue if I repyne,
   The fault is yours, & none of myne.

CANT. LXVII.

H. W.

I Will not wish, I cannot vow,
  Thy hurt, thy griefe, though thou disdaine,
  Though thou refuse, I know not how,
To quite my loue with loue againe:
    Since I haue swore to be thy frend,
    As I began, so will I end.

Sweare thou my death, worke thou my woe,
Conspire with greefe to stop my breath,
Yet still thy frend, & not thy foe
I will remayne vntill my death:
    Choose whome thou wilt, I will resigne,
    If loue, or faith, be like to mine.

But while I wretch too long haue lent
My wandering eyes to gase on thee.
I haue both tyme, & trauell spent
In vaine, in vaine: and now I see,
    They do but frutelesse paine procure,
    To haggard kytes that cast the lure. / [P 56 a

When I am dead, yet thou mayst boast,
Thou hadst a frend, a faithfull frend,
That liuing liu'd to loue thee most,
And lou'd thee still vnto his end:
　　Though thou vnworthy, with disdaine
　　Did'st force him liue, and dye in paine.

Now may I sing, now sigh, and say,
Farewell my lyfe, farewell my ioy,
Now mourne by night, now weepe by day,
Loue, too much loue breedes myne annoy:
　　What can I wish, what should I craue,
　　Sith that is gon, that I should haue.

Though hope be turned to dispaire,
Yet giue my tongue leaue to lament,
Beleeue me now, my hart doth sweare,
My lucklesse loue was truly ment:
　　Thou art too proud, I say no more,
　　Too stout, and wo is me therefore.
　　　　　　　　　　　Felice chi puo.

CANT. LXVIII.

Auisa hauing heard this patheticall fancy of
H. W. and seeing the teares trill downe his cheekes,
as halfe angry to see such passionate follie, in a
man that should haue gouerment, with a frowning

countenance turned from him, without farder answere, making silence her best reply, and following the counsell of the wise, not to answere a foole in his folly lest he grow too foolish, returted quite from him, and left him alone. But he departing home, and not able by reason to rule the raginge fume of this phantasticall fury, cast himselfe vppon his / bed, & refusing both foode & comfort for [56b many daies together, fell at length into such extremity of passionate affections, that as many as saw him, had great doubt of his health, but more of his wittes, yet, after a long space a bsence, hauing procured some respite from his sorrowes, he takes his pen & wrate, as followeth.

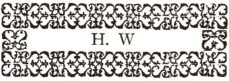

H. W

L Yke wounded Deare, whose tēder sydes are bath'd
in blood,
From deadly wound, by fatall hand & forked
shaft:
So bleedes my pearced hart, for so you thinke it good,
With cruelty to kill, that which you got by craft:
You still did loth my lyfe, my death shall be your
gaine,
To dye to do you good, I shall not thinke it paine.

My person could not please, my talke was out of frame,
Though hart and eye could neuer brooke my loathed
sight,
Yet loue doth make me say, to keepe you out of blame,
The fault was only mine, and that you did but right,
When I am gon, I hope my ghost shall shew you
plaine,
That I did truly loue, and that I did not faine.

Now must I fynd the way to waile while lyfe doth last,
Yet hope I soone to see, the end of dolefull dayes;
When floudes of flowing feares, and creeping cares are
past,
Then shall I leaue to sing, and write these pleasant
layes:
For now I loth the foode, and bloud that lendes me
breath,
I count all pleasures paine that keepe me from my
death. | [57 a

To darke and heauy shades, I now will take my flight,
Where nether tongue nor eye shall tell or see my fall,
That there I may disiect these dregges of thy dispight,
And purge the clotted blood, that now my hart doth
gall:
In secret silence so, Perforce *shall be my song,*
Till truth make you confesse that you haue done me
wrong.
                              Gia speme spenta.
                                    H. W.

Auisa refusing both to come or send him any aunswere, after a long & melancholike deliberation, he wrate againe so as followeth.

C A N T. LXIX

H. W.

THough you refuse to come or send,
   Yet this I send, though I do stay,
   Vnto these lynes some credit lend,
And marke it well what they shall say,
   They cannot hurt, then reade them all,
   They do but shew their maisters fall.

Though you disdaine to shew remorce,
You were the first and onely wight,
Whose fawning features did inforce
My will to runne beyond my might:
   In femall face such force we see,
   To captiue them, that erst were free. / [57b

Your onely word was then a law
Vnto my mynd, if I did sinne,
Forgiue this sinne, but then I saw
My bane or blisse did first beginnne,
  See what my fancy coulde haue donne,
  Your loue at first, if I had wonne.

All fortune flat I had defyde,
To choice and change defyance sent,
No frowning fates could haue denyde,
My loues pursute, & willing bent,
  This was my mynd, if I had found
  Your loue as myne, but halfe so sound.

Then had I bad the hellish rout,
To frounce aloft their wrinckled front,
And cursed haggs that are so stout,
I boldly would haue bid auaunt,
  Let earth and ayre haue fround their fill,
  So I had wrought my wished will.

No raging storme, nor whirling blast,
My setled heart could haue annoyd,
No sky with thundering cloudes orecast
Had hurt, if you I had enioyd,
  Now hope is past, loe you may see,
  How euery toy tormenteth mee.

                    Chi cerca troua. / [58a

CANT. LXX.

H. W.

Ith oken planckes to plane the waues,
What Neptunes rage could I haue fear'd
To quell the gulfe that rudely raues,
What perill could haue once appear'd?
    But now that I am left alone;
    Bare thoughts enforce my hart to grone.

With thee to passe the chamfered groundes,
What force or feare could me restraine?
With thee to chase the Scillan houndes,
Me thinkes it were a pleasant paine,
    This was my thought, this is my loue,
    Which none but death, can yet remoue.

It then behoues my fainting sprite,
To lofty skyes returne againe,
Sith onely death bringes me delite,
Which louing liue in curelesse paine,
    VVhat hap to strangers is assind,
    If knowne frendes doo such fauour find.

L

How often haue my frendly mates
My louing errours laught to scorne,
How oft for`thee found I debates,
VVhich now I wish had beene forborne:
  But this & more would I haue donne,
  If I thy fauour could haue wonne. | [58b

I saw your gardens passing fyne,
VVith pleasant flowers lately dect,
With Couslops and with Eglentine,
When wofull Woodbyne lyes reiect:
  Yet these in weedes and briars meet,
  Although they seeme to smell so sweet.

The dainty Daysy brauely springes,
And cheefest honour seemes to get,
I enuy not such frendly thinges,
But blesse the hand that these haue set:
  Yet let the Hysope haue his place,
  That doth deserue a speciall grace.
                    Viui, Chi vince.

CANT. LXXI.

H. W.

BVt now farewell, your selfe shall see,
An odd exchange of frends in tyme,
you may perhappes then wish for mee,
And waile too late this cruell cryme:
Yea wish your selfe perhaps beshrewd,
That you to me such rigor shewd.

I cannot force you for to like,
Where cruell fancy doth rebell,
I must some other fortune seeke,
But where or how I cannot tell:
And yet I doubt where you shall find
In all your life so sure a friend. | [59a

Of pleasant dayes the date is donne,
My carcase pyneth in conceat,
The lyne of lyfe his race hath runne,
Expecting sound of deathes retreat:
Yet would I liue to loue thee still,
And do thee good against thy will.

How can I loue, how can I liue,
Whil'st that my hart hath lost his hope,
Dispaire abandons sweet reliefe,
My loue, and life haue lost their scope:
   Yet would I liue thy feature to behold,
   Yet would I loue, if I might be so bold.

These
verses ex-
ceed mea-
sure, to
shew that
his affec-
tions
keepe no
compasse,
and his
exceeding
loue.

My griefe is greene, and neuer springes,
My sorrowe full of deadly sap,
Sweet death remoue these bitter thinges,
Giue end to hard and cruell hap:
   Yet would I liue, if I might see,
   My life, or limmes might pleasure thee.

Farewell that sweet and pleasant walke,
The witnesse of my faith and wo,
That oft hath heard our frendly talke,
An giu'n me leaue my griefe to show,
   O pleasant path, where I could see
   No crosse at all but onely shee.

Il fine, fa il tutto. / [59*b*

CANT. LXXII.

H. W.

Ike silly Bat, that loues the darke,
And seldome brookes the wished light,
Obscurely so I seeke the marke,
That aye doth vanish from my sight,
Yet shall she say, I died her frend,
Though by disdaine she sought mine end.

Faine would I cease, and hold my tong,
But loue and sorrow set me on,
Needes must I plaine of spitefull wrong,
Sith hope and health will both be gon,
   When branch from inward rind is fled,
   The barke doth wish the body dead.

If euer man were borne to woe,
I am the man, you know it well,
My chiefest friend, my greatest foe,
And heauen become my heauie hell,
   This do I feele, this do I find:
   But who can loose, that God will bind?

For since the day, O dismall day,
I first beheld that smiling face,
My fancie made her choice straightway,
And bad all other loues giue place,
    Yea since I saw thy louely sight,
    I frize and frie, twixt ioye and spight. | [Q 60a

Where fond suspect doth keepe the gate,
There trust is chased from the dore,
Then faith and truth will come too late,
Where falshod will admit no more;
    Then naked faith and loue must yeeld,
    For lacke offence, and flie the feeld.

Then easier were it for to chuse,
To crale against the craggie hill,
Then sutes, then sighs, then words to vse,
To change a froward womans will,
    Then othes and vowes are all in vaine,
    And truth a toye, where fancies raigne.

                    Ama, Chi ti ama.

CANT. LXXIII.

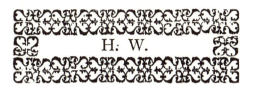

H: W.

M Y tongue, my hand, my ready hart,
  That spake, that felt, that freely thought,
My loue, thy limbes, my inward smart,
Haue all performed what they ought,
  These all do loue you yet, and shall,
  And when I change, let vengeance fall.

Shall I repent, I euer saw
That face, that so can frowne on mee?
How can I wish, when fancies draw
Mine eies to wish, and looke for thee?
  Then though you do denie my right,
  Yet bar me not from wished sight. | [60b

And yet I craue, I know not what,
Perchance my presence breeds your paine,
And if I were perswaded that,
I would in absence still remaine,
  You shall not feele the smallest griefe,
  Although it were to saue my life,

Ah woe is me, the case so stands,
That sencelesse papers plead my wo,
They can not weepe, nor wring their hands,
But say perhaps, that I did so,
 And though these lines for mercie craue,
 Who can on papers pittie haue?

O that my griefes, my sighs, my teares,
Might plainely muster in your vew,
Then paine, not pen, then faith, not feares,
Should vouch my vowes, and writings trew,
 This wishing shewes a wofull want,
 Of that which you by right should grant.

Now fare thou well, whose wel-fare brings
Such lothsome feare, and ill to me.
Yet heere thy friend this farwell sings,
Though heauie word a farwell be.
 Against all hope, if I hope still,
 Blame but abundance of good will.

Grand Amore, grand Dolore,
Inopem me copia fecit.
 H. W. / [61*a*

CANT, LXXIIII.

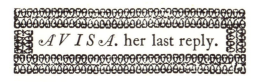

AVISA. her last reply.

Our long Epistle I haue read,
Great store of words, and little wit,
(For want of wit, these fancies bred)
To aunswere all I thinke not fit,
 But in a word, you shall perceaue,
 How kindly I will take my leaue.

When you shall see sweete Lillies grow,
And flourish in the frozen yse,
When ebbing tides shall leaue to flow,
And mountaines to the skies shall ryse,
 When roring Seas do cease to raue,
 Then shall you gaine the thing you craue.

When Fish as haggard Hawkes shall flie,
When Seas shall flame, and Sunne shall freese,
When mortall men shall neuer die,
And earth shall yeeld, nor herbe nor trees,
 Then shall your words my mind remoue,
 And I accept your proffered loue.

When Thames shall leaue his channell drie,
When Sheepe shall feede amidst the Sea.
When stones aloft, as Birds shall flie,
And night be changed into Day,
   Then shall you see that I will yeeld,
   And to your force resigne the feeld. | [61*b*

Till all these things doe come to passe,
Assure your selfe, you know my mind,
My hart is now, as first it was,
I came not of dame Chrysiedes *kind,*
   Then leaue to hope, learne to refraine,
   Your mind from that, you seeke in vaine.

I wish you well, and well to fare,
And there with all a godly mind,
Deuoid of lust, and foolish care,
This if you seeke, this shall you find.
   But I must say, as erst before,
   Then cease to waile, and write no more.

Alway the same
Auisa.

H. W. Was now againe striken so dead, that hee
hath not yet any farder assaid, not I thinke euer
will, and where he be aliue or dead I know not, and
therfore I leaue him. | [62*a*

The Authors conclusion.

SO thus she stands vnconquered yet,
 As Lambe amidst the Lions pause,
 Whom gifts, nor wils, nor force of wit,
  Could vanquish once with all their shewes,
To speake the truth, and say no more,
 I neuer knew her like before.

Then blame me not, if I protest,
My sillie Muse shall still commend
This constant A. aboue the rest,
While others learne their life to mend,
 My tongue on high and high shall raise,
 And alway sing her worthie praise.

While hand can write, while wit deuise,
While tongue is free to make report,
Her vertue shall be had in prise
Among the best and honest sort,
 And they that wil mislike of this,
 I shall suspect, they strike amis.

Eternall then let be the fame
Of such as hold a constant mind,
Eternall be the lasting shame,
Of such as waue with euery wind:
 Though some there be that will repine;
 Yet some will praise this wish of mine.

But here I cease for feare of blame,
Although there be a great deale more,
That might be spoken of this dame,
That yet lies hid in secret store,
    If this be lik't, then can I say,
    Ye may see more another day.

Agitante calescimus illo.

F I N I S.   Farewell. / [62*b*

The resolution of a chast and a con-
stant wife, that minds to continue
faithfull vnto her husband. To the
tune of Fortune.

THough winged Birds, do often skorne the lure,
And flying farre, do thinke them selues most sure,
Yet fancie so, his luring ingines frame,
That wildest harts, in time become most tame.

Where secret nature, frames a sweete consent,
Where priuie fates their hidden force haue bent,
To ioyne in hart, the bodies that are twaine,
Flie where you list, you shall returne againe.

From fancies lore, I striued still to flie,
Long time I did my fortune flat denie,
Till at the length, my wrastling bred my woe,
Knowing that none, their fortune can forgoe.

For while I liu'd, in prime of vernant youth,
Falshod that shew'd, the face of fained truth,
Falsly gan weaue, a web of wylie kind;
So to intrap, my plaine and simple mind.

Great were the sutes, great were the frendly signes,
Sweete were the words, to poyson tender minds,
Large were the gifts, great were the proffers made,
To force my mind, to trie a trustless trade.

Great were the wights, that dayly did conspire,
To pluck the rose, their fancies did desire,
Traile did the teares, in hope to purchase trust,
Yet this was all, no loue, but luring lust. /   [63a

No fancie could then force me to replie,
Nor moue my mind such doubtfull deeds to trie:
For well I knew, although I knew not all,
Such trickle trades procure a suddaine fall.

Thus did I mount, thus did I flie at will,
Thus did I scape the foulers painted skill,
Thus did I saue, my feathers from their lime,
Thus did I liue, a long and happie time.

Cupid that great, and mightie kings could moue,
Could neuer frame, my hart to like of loue,
His limber shafts, and eke his golden dart,
Were still too blunt, to pearce my steelie hart.

Till at the length, as nature had assind,
Vnto the earth, I bent a willing mind:
He was the first, to whom I gaue my hand,
With free consent, to liue in holy band.

Eua that gaue her faithfull promise so,
With Adam to liue in wealth and in wo,
Of faithfull hart, could neuer haue more store,
Then I haue felt, thrice three yeares space & more.

When I had gieu'n my hart and free consent,
No earthly thing could make me once repent,
No Seas of griefe, ne cares that I could find,
Could so preuaile, to make me change my mind.

Did fortune fawne, or did our fortune frowne,
Did he exalt, or did he cast him downe,
My faithfull hart did euer make me sing,
Welcome to me, what euer fortune bring.

Now when I thought, all dangers had bene past
Of lawlesse sutes, and sutors at the last,
The trade, the time, the place wherein I liue,
Vnto this Lampe, new oyle doe dayly giue. / [63*b*

But like of this all you that loue to range,
My fixed hart likes not the skittish change,
Now haue I made the choice that shall remaine,
Vengeance befall, when I do change againe.

Now haue I found a friend of high desart,
I haue his loue, and he hath stoole my hart,
Now fortune packe, with all thy pelting store,
This is my choice, I like to chuse no more

Cease then your sutes, yee lustie gallants all,
Thinke not I stoupe at euery Faulkners call,
Trusse vp your lures, your luring is in vaine,
Chosen is the Pearch, whereon I will remaine.

Spend not your breath in needlesse fained talkes,
Seeke other mates, that loue such rouing walkes,
None shall euer vaunt, that they haue my consent,
Then let me rest, for now I am content.

Great be your birth, and greater be your wealth,
I recken more my credit and my health,
Though I be weake, my power very scant,
God so prouides that I shal neuer want.

Be mine owne at home, or be he absent long,
Absent or present, this still shall be my song,
Fortune my friend, A friend to me hath lent,
This is my choise, and therewith am content.

Range they that list, and change who euer will,
One hath mine oth, and his I will be still,
Now let vs fall, or let vs rise on hie,
Still will I sing, now well content am I. / [R 64*a*

The praise of a contented mind.

THe God that framde the fixed pole, and Lamps of gleaming light,
The azure skies, and twinkling Starres, to yeeld this pleasant sight,
In wisdome pight this perelesse plot, a rare surpassing frame,
And so with braue and sweete delights, haue fraught and dect the same,
That euery creature keepes his course, his compasse and his place,
And with delightfull ioye runnes, his pointed time and race,
In one consent they friendly ioyne, from which they can not fall,
As if the Lord had first ordainde, one soule to guide them all,
In euery part there doth remaine, such loue and free consent,
That every frame doth kisse his lot, and cries I am content,
The Articke pole that neuer moues, by which the shipmen saile,
Craues not to change his frizen Axe, nor from his place to steale,
The fixed Starres, that sildome range, delight their circles so,
That from their choise by wanton change, they neuer yeeld to go.
The Sunne and Moone that neuer hide, their braue resplendent raics,
Did neuer wish in wauering will, to change their wonted waies.
The roaring Sea, with ebbs and tides, that leapes against the land,
Is yet content for all his rage, to stay within his band.
The flooting Fish, the singing Bird, all beasts with one consent,
To liue according to their kind, do shew them selues content.
So that by practise and by proofe, this sentence true I find,
That nothing in this earth is like, a sweete contended mind.

M

The beasts, the Birds, and ayrie powers, do keepe their compasse well,
And onely man aboue the rest, doth loue for to rebell,
This onely man, the Lord aboue, with reason did indue,
Yet onely man, vngratefull man, doth shew himselfe vntrue.
No sooner was braue Adam made, but Sathan wrought his thrall,
For not content, aspiring pride, procurde his suddaine fall.
The princely Primerose of the East, proud Eua gaue consent,
To change her bliss to bale, for that, her mind was not content.
Thus may the darkest eie perceiue, how follie strikes vs blind,
Thus may we see the often change, of mans vnconstant mind,
The Moone, the Sea, by natures course, do not so often change.
As do the wits, and wanton wils, of such as loue to range.
The rangling rage that held from home, Vlisses all too long,
Made chast Penelope complaine of him that did her wrong.
The lothsome daies, and lingering nights, her time in spinning spent:
She would not yeeld to change her choice, because she was content.
Such calme content doth plainely shew, that loue did much abound,
Where free consent breeds not content, such faith is seldome found.
For carelesse Crysed that had gin, her hand, her faith and hart,
To Troilus her trustie friend, yet falsely did depart.
And giglot like from Troye towne, to Grecians campe would goe, / [64b
To Diomede, whom in the end, she found a faithless foe,
For hauing sliu'd the gentle slip, his loue was turnd to hate.
And she a leaper did lament, but then it was too late.
Now foolish fancie was the cause, this Crysed did lament,
For when she had a faithfull friend, she could not be content.
Ten thousand fell at Troyes siege, whose bloud had not bene spent,
If fickle headded Hellen could, at first haue bene content.
You can not in the Serpents head, such deadly poyson find,
As is the fained loue that liues, with discontented mind.

Of all the wisdome of the wise, that I could euer tell,
This wisdome beares the chiefest sway, to stay when we be well,
As sweetest Musicke rudely iarres, except there be consent:
So hottest loue doth quickly coole, except it be content.
Of all the braue resounding words, which God to man hath lent,
This soundeth sweetest in mine eare, to say. *I am content.*

Euer or Neuer.

F I N I S.

LONDON
Imprinted by *Iohn Windet*, dwelling
at Pauls wharfe at the signe of the crosse
Keyes and are there to be solde.
1 5 9 4.

AN ESSAY ON
WILLOBIE HIS AVISA

By

GEORGE BAGSHAWE HARRISON

INTRODUCTORY

*W*ILLOBIE HIS AVISA is one of the most interesting of the minor problems of Elizabethan literature. The book tells the story of a certain woman of humble birth, whom the author designates by the name of 'Avisa'. She was the wife of an innkeeper, beautiful and witty, and, living always in the public eye, she attracted much notice. But with all her charms she combined an unassailable chastity—a virtue rare amongst hostesses, if contemporary pamphleteers are to be believed. Her suitors were many, and included noblemen, but all were rejected; and so 'Willobie', whoever he was, pens the praise of the chastity of a British matron, setting forth the petitions of her tempters and her replies in a series of cantos of mediocre verse.

This story, which seems to concern persons of far greater importance than the righteous Avisa, is interesting enough in itself, but it promises more. Amongst the suitors is a certain young man, H. W., who takes Avisa's refusal more hardly than the rest. In his misery he turns to his 'familiar frend W. S. who not long before had tryed the curtesy of the like passion'. W. S., 'in vewing a far off the course of this louing Comedy, he determined to see whether it would sort to a happier end for this new actor, then it did for the old player'. *Willobie His Avisa* was first printed in 1594; so was *Lucrece*, which William Shakespeare dedicated with much fervour to 'The Right Honourable Henry Wriothesley, Earl of Southampton, and Baron of Tichfield'. It is not surprising that critics should, like Sir Toby, 'smell a device', and that several attempts have been made to probe the mystery.

The problem, needless to say, is not easily solved. There are few clues in the book which are at all definite, and it is probable that there is a certain amount of intentional mystification. Hitherto attempts have been made mainly in two directions: by those who believe, with the late Sir Sidney Lee and the late Mr. Charles Hughes, that Henry Willobie is a real person; and by those who begin by assuming that 'W. S.' is Shakespeare and make Avisa one of the keys to the Sonnet problems. The chief exponent of this theory is

Mr. Arthur Acheson. Both theories will be briefly discussed later.

I have tried, so far as is possible in an inquiry of this kind, to be led by the evidence, and my method was first to study *Willobie His Avisa* by itself, without any reference to the literature on the subject or to other poems with which, rightly or wrongly, it has been connected. From internal evidence alone it seemed that Cerne Abbas in Dorsetshire was the starting point of my quest, and thither I went in the summer of 1925 to study the locality. What I found seemed to justify my belief, and led on to the very tentative conclusions expressed in this essay.

However, whether my conclusions have any value or not, I believe that students will welcome the complete transcript of the proceedings of the Inquiry which was held at Cerne Abbas in March 1594 to gather evidence of the atheism of Sir Walter Raleigh.

I would only make one appeal to my critics— that they will not read the conclusion before they read the essay.

I wish to express my grateful thanks to Dr. A. W. Pollard, Mr. Leslie E. Bliss, Acting Librarian of the Huntington Library, Mr. Vere S. Oliver, Mr. Arundell del Re, and the Rev. C. F. Hall, Rector of Cerne Abbas.

BIBLIOGRAPHY

The bibliographical history of the text is as follows:

1594. 3rd September, *Willobie His Avisa* was entered in the Stationers' Register—

> Master Windet Enterd for his copie vnder th[e h]andes of master HARTWELL and the wardens A book entituled. WILLO-BYE *his avisa or the true picture of a modest maid and of a chas[t]e and Constant wife* . . . vj^d [1]

> The first edition was published during the next six months. Five copies are known, one being in the British Museum.

1596. A certain Peter Colse published *Penelope's Complaint*, in which he refers to and answers Willobie's claims on the behalf of Avisa. *Penelope's Complaint* was entered on 13 February 1595–6. It is dedicated to Sir Ralph Horsey, Lord Lieutenant of Dorset, and Lady Horsey, and gives some information about Avisa's father which shows that she was known to Colse. The relevant passages will be found in Appendix I, on pp. 234–5.

Apparently another edition of *Willobie His Avisa* was brought out soon after. In the

---

[1] *Arber's Reprint*, ii. 659.

copy of the 1635 edition in the British
Museum there is a new Preface answering
Colse and a new poem (printed as Appendix
II on p. 245) which is dated 1569—an
obvious misprint for 1596. No copies of this
edition are known.

1599. To the list of books noted in the Stationers'
Register as burnt in the hall on 4 June is
added the note:

> 'Theis [were] stai[e]d [*i.e. not burnt*]
> *Caltha Poetarum*
> Halls *Satires*
> Willobies *Adviso* to be Called in.'[1]

Presumably a third edition was in print; but
no copies have survived.

1605. An edition, 'the fourth time corrected and
augmented', was published. A copy was in
the Britwell Court Sale in 1922.

1609. The fifth edition was published; a copy is
in the Henry E. Huntington Library, San
Gabriel, California.

1635. The sixth edition was published. There
are copies in the British Museum and
Huntington Libraries.

[1] *Ibid.* iii. 678.

GENERAL CONSIDERATIONS

Willobie His Avisa is, at first sight, the work of a young student of the highest moral principles. Such works are indeed written from time to time by young men from the university, but they are seldom published; seldomer do they reach a sixth edition. Moreover, the authorities disliked the book strongly, and there was doubtless good reason why, in June 1599, *Willobie His Avisa* should have been included in the category of books to be burned with such libellous and indecent works as *Pygmalion*, *The Scourge of Villainy*, Davies' *Epigrammes* and *The Fifteen Joys of Marriage*.

Willobie His Avisa, in short, is not what it pretends to be. The initials of Avisa's suitors covered, or rather revealed to contemporaries, persons of great importance; so great, in fact, that the scandals about them were still commercially worth retailing forty years later.

Now the great men of the early 1590's who were the butts of poets and pamphleteers were not very numerous, and usually they belonged to one or two quite well-known literary cliques. Moreover, those who were still great fifteen years later were even fewer.

Nevertheless, without some external clue, identification in this or any other Elizabethan poem is seldom certain. Few popular works of the decade are entirely without some secondary meaning. Usually the writer chose a theme which here and there bore resemblance to the times and which allowed for topical allusion, allegorical interpretation, or even deliberate digression. Few poems, however, can be directly translated into history. Spenser's Sir Artegall, with Talus his man of iron, figures the Irish administration of Lord Grey, yet, without the gloss, this fact would not be obvious in the story. *Midas* and *Endymion*, Lyly's Court comedies, are straightforward versions of quite familiar fables; at the same time, so Lyly's editors tell us, they are really political allegories. Even Nashe's *Piers Penilesse* is a reasonably consistent story on the familiar pattern of the Seven Deadly Sins, in spite of the fact that it alludes to nearly every piece of important gossip and includes a complete allegorical satire on the late Earl of Leicester's relations with the Martinists; whilst in *Mother Hubberds Tale* and the elegies for Astrophel it is difficult to separate fact from the pastoral and allegorical settings. In short, the Elizabethan reader was accustomed to look for a hidden meaning in most of the books which he read.

Nor in this story of *Willobie His Avisa* must the text be scrutinized too curiously; and herein lies the chief difficulty of attempting a solution. Each interpreter must decide for himself in any given passage whether the verse is part of the fable or one of the essential facts in the case. It is unlikely, on the face of it, that Avisa had so free a flow of Scriptural illustration, all ready to hand in rhymed stanzas, with which to overwhelm her adversaries, or further, that the cantos which bear her name do in any way reflect the language or sentiments even of this exceptional hostess. On the other hand, when she draws a discreditable conclusion from the 'wannie cheekes' and 'shaggie lockes' of 'Caveleiro', the remark seems likely enough, and is probably a very palpable hit at some definite person.

Nor, again, does it necessarily follow that H. W. ever met the real Avisa. It would be quite in keeping with the modes of Elizabethan allegorical satire for him to be brought into the book as her wooer if he were known to have had similar adventures elsewhere.

Nevertheless, great though the difficulties are, the problem is not, perhaps, insoluble; and the first step is to see what 'Willobie' has to say about 'Avisa'.

AVISA

The first canto of the book is concerned with the birth and habitation of Avisa. Allowing for the licence of a minor poet and deliberate falsification, certain quite definite hints are given, and it should be possible to identify Avisa—if the local records are in existence!

It is stated that the Graces met to compound Avisa

> At wester side of Albions Ile, (23: 7)[1]
> Where Austine pitcht his Monkish tent.

These words might refer to any place where Austin (i.e. St. Augustine) settled in his wanderings in the West, but the obvious identification is with Cerne Abbas in Dorsetshire, where Augustine founded the Abbey, and where his sacred well can still be seen.

Camden, in his *Britannia*, remarks: '. . . Cerne Abbey; which *Augustine* the Apostle of the English nation built, when hee had broken there in pieces, *Heil* the Idol of the heathen English-Saxons, and chased away the fog of paganish superstition'.[2]

[1] For convenience of reference the first figure refers to the page, the second to the line of the present reprint.

[2] Camden's *Britain*, translated by Philemon Holland, 1637, f. 212.

Fuller has a more picturesque account: 'Another considerable Accession was made to Christianity in the South-West part of this Ile, and particularly in *Dorsetshire*; where *Augustine* at *Cern*, destroyed the Idol of *Heale* or *Æsculapius*, which the *Saxons* formerly adored. But in his journey hither (Reader, they are not mine, but my Authours words) *with his Holy Company, they were cruelly oppressed with the three familiar Discommodities of Travellers, Hunger, Thirst, and Wearinesse; when* Augustine *striking his Staffe into the Ground, fetch'd forth a crystal Fountain, which quenched the extremity of their Thirst: whence the Place was afterward called* Cernel, *from* Cerno *in* Latine, *to see, and* El *in* Hebrew, *God*. A Composition of a Name hardly to be precedented, that a Word should commence *per saltum*, from *Latine* into *Hebrew*, without taking *Greek* by the way thereof. Why not rather *Cernwell, Behold the fountain*; or *Cernheal, See the Destruction of the Idol?* But in truth, in all Books ancient and modern, the Place is plainly written *Cern*, without any paragogical apposition thereunto.'[1]

Cerne Abbas is now an agricultural village; in former times it was of some local importance, and visitors are still shown the site of a leather-seller's

[1] *The Church History of Britain*, 1655, Book II, 66–7.

shop where Sir Walter Raleigh used to buy his gloves and jerkins. The Abbey suffered at the Reformation, but a magnificent gateway and the guest-house still remain, neglected and rapidly falling to pieces in a farmyard.

The Registers of Cerne begin in 1653, and some parish accounts go back to 1632.

There is external evidence to support this locality as the birthplace of Avisa. The fact that Peter Colse's *Penelope's Complaint*, avowedly an answer to *Willobie His Avisa*, is dedicated to Sir Ralph Horsey and his Lady, the tone of the dedication itself, and especially the Latin verses of 'S. D.', strongly suggest that Sir Ralph himself had some personal feeling about Avisa.[1]

Sir Ralph Horsey, one of the most important landowners in Dorsetshire at the time, was appointed Lord Lieutenant of the County on 31 January 1592. He lived at Melcombe Horsey, some six miles to the east of Cerne.

———————

Mr. Arthur Acheson has claimed Avisa as the wife of John Davenant, an Oxford innkeeper, father of Sir William Davenant, the Restoration dramatist. Aubrey says of the Davenants: 'Mr. William Shakespeare was wont to goe into

[1] See Appendix I, pp. 234–5.

Warwickshire once a yeare, and did commonly in his journey lye at this house in Oxon. where he was exceedingly respected. I^d have heard parson Robert [Davenant] say that Mr. W. Shakespeare haz given him a thousand kisses. Now Sir William would sometimes, when he was pleasant over a glasse of wine with his most intimate friends— e.g. Sam. Butler (author of Hudibras), &c.—say, that it seemed to him that he writt with the very spirit that Shakespeare, and seemd contented enough to be thought his son. He would tell the story as above, in which way his mother had a very light report.'[1]

Mr. Acheson holds that the 'Davenant Scandal' is a confused recollection of the scandals recorded in *Willobie His Avisa* and Shakespeare's *Sonnets*. His argument is that John Davenant must have married a lady whose surname was Anne; this lady, he claims, was not only Avisa (A. D.), but also the Dark Lady of the Sonnets. 'A. D.', however, was not Sir William Davenant's mother; her name was Jane, and she was married in 1602—eight years after the publication of *Willobie His Avisa*. Mr. Acheson therefore suggests that Jane was blameless, but has been confused with a previous Mrs. Davenant. The facts about John Davenant can be

[1] *Aubrey's Brief Lives.* Edited by A. C. Clark, i. 204.

most fairly summarised in Mr. Acheson's own words:[1]

'John Davenant—later of Oxford—son of John Davenant, junior, was baptised on August 6, 1565, in the Parish Church of St. Thomas the Apostle, was entered at the Merchant Taylors' School in 1574, and was apprenticed to Robert Kendrick in 1581, and secured the Freedom of the Company in 1589. Between this latter date and 1602, when the birth of his first child is recorded in the Registers of St. Martin's at Oxford, I have so far been unable to find any actual record of his name. I possess, however, conclusive circumstantial evidence showing that he married Anne Sackfielde, illegitimate daughter of Mayor William Bird, of Bristol, in 1591-2, and that he subleased from William Rough for a period of forty years the tavern adjoining the Crosse Inn at Oxford; this tavern at that time bearing no specific name and being regarded as an adjunct of the Crosse Inn. He died in 1622 . . .

'In the records of the burials in Westminster Abbey, in a footnote concerning the burial of Sir William Davenant, I learn that his mother was a Jane Shepherd, of Durham. John Davenant's first

[1] In a letter contributed to *The Times Literary Supplement* of 28 July 1921.

N

wife must have died before 1600 to 1601, when he married his second wife, as divorces were then unobtainable.'

Mr. Acheson's arguments are developed at considerable length in his *Shakespeare's Sonnet Story* and previous works, and there is no space here to criticise them in detail. Seeing that nothing is known of John Davenant between 1589 and 1602, he is perhaps optimistic in claiming that the circumstantial evidence for Davenant's unhappy marriage with Anne Sackfield and her subsequent death is 'conclusive'.

On more general grounds, however, there seems to be no reason to identify Avisa with the Dark Lady of the Sonnets, for they have nothing in common. The one fact that is known about the Dark Lady is that she was dark; there is no suggestion of darkness about Avisa. The main facts that are known about Avisa are that she was the wife of an innkeeper and the daughter of an innkeeper; there is no suggestion that the Dark Lady served in an inn.

AVISA'S DWELLING

Avisa, we are told, married an innkeeper, and the band of her admirers increased

'When flying fame began to tell,
   How beauties wonder was returnd,
   From countrie hils, in towne to dwell.' (28 : 7)

Cerne lies in a valley surrounded by rolling downs. The 'town' where Avisa dwelt after her marriage is—

(a) 'Not farre from thence' [*i.e. her birth-place*].

(b) In 'a rosie vale in pleasant plaine' (26: 1)

(c) 'At East of this, a Castle stands,
   By auncient sheepheards built of olde,
   And lately was in sheepheards hands,
   Though now by brothers bought and solde.'
   (26: 7)

(d) 'At west side springs a Christall well.'
   (26: 11)

(e) 'She dwels in publique eye' (26: 13) at an inn which H. W. indicates to W. S. as
   'Seest yonder howse, where hanges the badge
   Of Englands Saint, when captaines cry
   Victorious land, to conquering rage,
   Loe, there my hopelesse helpe doth ly.'
   (121: 1)

There are two towns near Cerne: Dorchester seven miles to the south, Sherborne eleven to the north. Sherborne fulfils most of the conditions:

(*a*) It is 'not far from thence', and communication between Cerne and Sherborne was frequent.

(*b*) Sherborne lies in the Blackmore Vale: it is, as a glance at the raised map of Dorsetshire will show, very noticeably in a vale in a plain. Sheep still graze on the downs.

(*c*) On the East stand the remains of the Norman Castle which was originally built by Bishop Roger le Rich, Chancellor to Henry I, and remained the property of the Bishops of Salisbury ('ancient shepherds') until the Reformation. The castle was granted to Sir Walter Raleigh by Queen Elizabeth in 1592. The reference to brothers I have not been able to trace, but it should be noted that there were two very famous brothers living in the castle at the time—Sir Walter and Mr. Carew Raleigh, who were engaged in building operations in 1594.

(*d*) At the West of the town rises the Newell or New Well spring, which at one time supplied the Abbey but is now used to fill the swimming bath of Sherborne School.

(*e*) The old George Inn, one of the oldest inns in the town, stands at the top of Cheap

Street. Its original front has been replaced, but the gateway into the yard still remains.

AVISA'S AGE

Avisa is apparently twenty-nine years old. 'Full twenty years she lived a maid' (27: 17), and she has been married 'thrice three yeares space & more' (175: 4). If these statements are correct—though one must not be too exacting over such details—Avisa was born about 1565 and married about 1585; she was quite old enough to look after herself.

AVISA'S NAME

Hadrian Dorrell seems to suggest that Avisa's initials are A. D. (10: 4); but it does not necessarily follow: he might have been thinking of one of his own relations. It is, moreover, probable from the number of references to birds, falconers, lures, and so forth, that Avisa's name has some connection with a bird. It may be that her surname was Bird, Hawke, Falcon or the like; but if so, 'Avisa' is a curious Latinism, even for a cryptic poem. More likely Avisa is the Latinised form of Avis, a Christian name fairly common in

Sherborne at the time. In the Abbey Registers, for instance, it is recorded that in 1588 Thomas Gaffe married Avis Andrews on 21 October. On 27 December, Avis Oke was buried. On 2 February 1590, John Barlow married Avis Marchant.

It is not very probable that Avisa was married at Sherborne. If she was, Anne Hauken, who married Henry Marten (both bird names!) on 22 August 1588 might be a claimant, especially as a child, apparently their daughter, was baptized on 15 April 1592 and given the name of Avis. Unfortunately, the Sherborne Registers are regrettably brief and do not give the names of parents in the lists of baptisms.

AVISA'S RELATIONS

Avisa's father was an innkeeper, '*Avisa Coniux cauponis, filia pandochei*' (235: 1). He was 'Maior of the towne' (27: 15). There were no mayors of Cerne or Sherborne, but the title might reasonably refer to anyone holding an office (such as reeve, high bailiff or the like) which corresponded.[1]

[1] It might conceivably be a nickname. Whilst at Cerne Abbas last summer I made inquiries for the names of those who were authorities on local history, and was directed to a gentleman who is known locally as the 'Mayor of Cerne'.

Avisa's husband was also an innkeeper, but in the absence of local records I have not been able to trace the innkeepers of Sherborne at the time.

These local references, then, point to a fairly strong probability that Avisa lived in the neighbourhood of Cerne in Dorsetshire; that she was the hostess at an inn; and that her reputation as a paragon of virtue was considerable, unless, indeed, as has been suggested, the 'chaste Avisa' was notoriously wanton.

SIR WALTER RALEIGH AND SHERBORNE

Though some way from the capital, Sherborne was likely to be well known to Londoners. It was one of the stages on the regular route to Plymouth, and the reputation of the beautiful hostess of the George might well reach London and be comparable with the fame of 'mine host at Saint Alban's or the red-nosed innkeeper of Daventry.' More important still, Sherborne was the home of Sir Walter Raleigh.

It is not irrelevant, then, to consider some of the events which happened in the neighbourhood of Sherborne, or which concerned its chief

inhabitant in the period immediately preceding
the publication of *Willobie His Avisa*.

At the beginning of 1592, Raleigh was at the
height of his success. He was Captain of the
Guard, in immediate attendance on the Queen's
person, and therefore a most important official in
Court circles. But 'he was damnably proud'.
'An old acquaintance and political ally, the Earl
of Northumberland, similarly describes Ralegh
as " insolent, extremely heated, a man that desired
to seem to be able to sway all men's courses."
That this was the current opinion, due, as it was,
more or less, to misconception, is borne out by a
mass of authority. Ralegh must have profoundly
impressed all about him with a sense that he felt
himself better fitted than themselves to regulate
their lives. His air of conscious superiority
silenced opposition, but was resented. Neither a
mob, nor Howards and Percies, pardoned his
assumption of an infinite superiority of capacity.
His gaiety and splendour were treated as proofs of
arrogance. His evident contempt of " the rascal
multitude " added to the odium which dogged his
course. He never condescended to allude to the
subject in writing or in authenticated speech.
Though he courted occasions for renown, he did
not seek applause. His position as a Queen's

favourite in any case must have brought aversion upon him.'[1] Raleigh, in short, was the best hated man in England, except in the West Country, where he was almost adored.

In January 1592 the Queen granted Raleigh the estate of Sherborne. 'It had belonged to the see of Salisbury since the time of Bishop Osmund, who cursed all who should alienate it, or profit by its alienation. Ralegh was not deterred by the threat. He is rumoured to have been impressed by the charms of the domain as he rode past it on his journeys from Plymouth to London. Towards the close of 1591 the bishopric of Salisbury, which had been vacant for three years, was filled by the appointment of Dr. Coldwell. Dean Bennett, of Windsor, and Dr. Tobias Matthew, or Matthews, afterwards Bishop of Durham and Archbishop of York, father to the wit and letter-writer, Sir Toby, had declined it on account of a condition that the new Bishop must consent to part with Sherborne. Ralegh subsequently declared that he had given the Queen a jewel worth £250 "to make the Bishop". He not rarely concerned himself about vacant bishoprics for his own purposes. His present fit of ecclesiastical zeal was explained by Dr. Coldwell's execution of a lease to the Crown in January 1592

[1] W. Stebbing, *Sir Walter Ralegh*. Oxford, 1899, p. 58.

of Sherborne and its dependencies for ninety-nine years. A rent was reserved to the see of £260, which, according to the Bishop, was not regularly paid. The Queen at once assigned the lease to Ralegh.'[1]

In the early part of the year, Raleigh had organized, and to a large extent financed, an expedition which was intended to cut out the Spanish Plate Fleet. The expedition was ready to put out to sea in May with Raleigh himself in command, but on the day after sailing, orders were received that he was to leave his command and to return forthwith. These orders he did not obey for four days. When he reached London, in June, he was at once thrown into the Tower; for he had committed the unpardonable sin, as Camden tersely remarks, 'honoraria Reginæ virgine vitiata, quam postea in uxorem duxit'. The offence, as Raleigh admitted, was 'brutish', and the Queen was justly enraged by this scandal in her own private apartments. Moreover, her personal vanity had received a terrible wound, for Raleigh's flatteries of his Virgin Mistress had been notoriously gross even for a courtier.

Raleigh's fall was a political event of the greatest importance; it removed the only ob-

[1] Stebbing, p. 101.

stacle to the ascendancy of the Earl of Essex and his faction.

Though confined to the Tower, Raleigh was not kept a close prisoner: his own servants attended him, and he was able to direct his private affairs. Release came unexpectedly. The expedition had succeeded beyond hope, and on the 8th September the fleet returned to Plymouth with the *Madre de Dios*, the 'great carrack', the richest prize ever brought into England by Elizabethan seamen. Immediately they reached port, the sailors began to plunder. The share-holders in the venture were naturally alarmed, and Sir Robert Cecil, with full powers, was despatched post haste to deal with the situation. He was followed a few days later by Raleigh, who was rightly considered the only person of sufficient influence with the men of Devon to restore order. He was still a prisoner under open arrest.

A commission consisting of Cecil, Raleigh and William Killigrew was appointed, and by their efforts most of the plunder was recovered. The proceeds were then shared out. The Queen was entitled to a return of about £20,000 on the money she had invested; Raleigh, as chief sharer, to much more. But he was in no position to bargain. He made a present to the Queen of about £80,000, and was allowed to retire to Sherborne. He was still exiled from Court, but otherwise his movements were not restricted, and during the months which followed he spent some time in London. He took a prominent part in the proceedings of the Parliament of 1593, and made a noteworthy speech on the dangers of religious intolerance.

With other great men of the time, Raleigh was a generous patron of scholars and men of letters, but his tastes were unconventional and his protégés were usually men of unorthodox and exceptional abilities. His coterie included Henry Percy, Earl of Northumberland, George Chapman, Christopher Marlowe, Matthew Roydon, and Thomas Harriott, one of the greatest of English mathematicians. Naturally the orthodox shook their heads at the discussions which went on, and the authorities too were not a little alarmed. 'Heresy' was a very real danger in the state at a time when the revolutionary spirit expressed itself in religious forms. The Jesuits were very active: only the year before an edict had been issued to deal with them. Moreover, the country had not yet recovered from the excitement of the Martinist pamphlets. Still, however misguided, popery and anti-prelacy were at least connected with the Bible: what sinister import might there not be in the discussions of a society which openly made a jest of Moses and the Holy Scriptures?

Raleigh's rival, the Earl of Essex, and his young friend, the Earl of Southampton, also patronised literary men, amongst whom were Thomas Nashe and William Shakespeare. To Southampton Nashe dedicated *The Unfortunate Traveller*, Barnabe Barnes included a complimentary sonnet in *Parthenope and Parthenophile*, and Shakespeare dedicated *Venus and Adonis* and *Lucrece*. It would seem that Southampton had not the same scientific tastes as Raleigh.

Now that Raleigh had fallen, he became fair game for wits. Nashe, in *Pierce Penilesse* (entered 8 August 1592), inserts a couple of paragraphs. 'An other misery of Pride it is, when men that haue good parts, and beare the name of deepe scholers: cannot be content to participate one faith with all Christendome, but because they will get a name to their vaineglory, they will set their selfe-loue to studie to inuent new sects of singularitie, thinking to liue when they are dead, by hauing sects called after their names, as *Donatists* of *Donatus*, *Arrians* of *Arrius*: and a number more new faith-founders that haue made *England* the exchange of Innouations, and almost as much confusion of Religion in euery quarter, as there was of tongues at the building of the Tower of *Babell.* Whence, a number that fetch the Articles of their Beleefe out of *Aristotle*, and thinke of heauen and hell as the Heathen Philosophers, take occasion to deride our Ecclesiasticall State, and all Ceremonies of Deuine worship, as bugbeares, scar-crowes, because (like *Herodes* souldiers) we diuide Christs garment amongst vs in so many peeces, and of the vesture of saluation make some of vs Babies and apes coates, others straight trusses and Diuells breeches: some gally-gascoines or a shipmans hose like the Anabaptists and adulterous Familists, others with the Martinist a hood with two faces to hide their hypocrisie: & to conclude some like the Barrowists and Greenwoodians, a garment full of the plague, which is not to be worne before it be new washt.

'Hence Athiests triumph and reioyce, and talke as prophanely of the Bible, as of Beuis of Hampton. I heare say there be Mathematicians abroad, that will prooue men before *Adam*, and they are harboured in high places, who will maintaine it to the death, that there are no diuels.'[1]

[1] *Pierce Penilesse His Supplication to the Diuell.* The Bodley Head Quartos, Vol. XI, p. 27. (In Dr. McKerrow's *Nashe*, vol. i, p. 171.)

Nashe returns to the charge in more general terms in *Christs Teares over Jerusalem* (entered 8 September 1593):

'The outwarde Athiest (contrariwise), with those thinges that proceede from his mouth, defileth hys hart; He establisheth reason as his God, and will not be perswaded that God (the true God) is, except he make him priuie to al the secrecies of his beginning & gouernment. Straightly he will examine hym where hee was, what he did, before he created Heauen and Earth; how it is possible hee should haue his beeing before all beginnings. Euery circumstance of his prouidence hee will runne through, and question why he did not thys thing, and that thing, and the other thing, according to theyr humors?'[1]

In 1592, Fr. Robert Parsons, under the pseudonym of 'D. Andreas Philopater', wrote a *Responsio ad Elizabethæ Edictum*, a commentary on the edict of 1591 directed against Catholics. He says:

'Et certè si Gualteri quoque Raulæi schola frequens de Atheismo paulo longius processerit, (quam modo ita notam & publicam suis in ædibus habere dicitur, Astronomo quodã necromãtico

---

[1] *The Works of Thomas Nashe.* Edited by Dr. R. B. McKerrow, Vol. ii, p. 118.

præceptore; vt iuuentutis nobilioris non exiguæ
turmæ, tam Moysis legem veterem, quàm nouam
Christi Domini, ingeniosis quibusdã facetijs ac
dicterijs eludere, ac in circulis suis irridere didi-
cerint, si hæc inquam schola radices ac robur
cæperit, & ipse Raulæus in senatum delectus
fuerit, quo reipub. quoque negotijs præsideat
(quod omnes non sine summa ratione expectãt,
cum primas apud Reginã post Dudlæum &
Hathonũ teneat, & ex gregario propè Hiberniæ
milite virum principem ac potẽtem Reginæ sola
gratia nullis præcedentibus meritis effectũ vi-
deant) quid (inquam) erit expectandum aliud nisi
vt aliquãdo etiam edictum aliquod a Màgo illo
atque Epicuro Raulæi præceptore cõscriptum
Reginæ nomine euuulgatũ cernamus, quo planè
omnis Diuinitas, omnis animæ immortalitas, &
alterius vitæ expectatio dilucidè, clarè, breuiter,
& citra ambages denegetur, & læsæ maiestatis
accusentur, tanquam reipub. perturbatores, qui
contra istiusmodi doctrinam tam placidam ac in
carnis vitijs volutantibus suauem, scrupulos cuiquã
alit molestias moueant.'[1]

Shortly after, a summary of the *Responsio* was
issued in English under the title of *An Advertise-
ment written to a Secretarie of my L. Treasurers of*

[1] p. 36.

Ingland, by an Inglish Intelligencer as he passed through Germanie towardes Italie. The book was printed abroad and was a cunning attempt to circulate the *Responsio* in the innocent guise of a warning to Protestants. The paragraph about Raleigh is summarized thus:

'Of Sir VValter Rauleys schoole of Atheisme by the waye, and of the Conjurer that is M. thereof, and of the dilegẽce vsed to get young gentlemẽ to this schoole, where in both Moyses, and our Sauior; the olde, and new Testamente are iested at, and the schollers taught amonge other thinges, to spell God backwarde.'[1]

It is probable also that the Raleigh group came in for a large share of the ridicule in Shakespeare's *Loves Labors Lost*[2] (? 1593), wherein Don Adriano de Armado has a strong family likeness to Raleigh, and Holofernes to Harriot.

The charges of unorthodoxy were not confined to Raleigh and Harriot; the other members of the circle were included. Thus, just before his death on 2nd September 1592, Robert Greene, in the famous letter 'To those Gentlemen his Quondam

[1] p. 18.

[2] See the Introduction to this play in *The New Shakespeare*, edited by Sir A. T. Quiller Couch and J. Dover Wilson.

o

acquaintance,'[1] called on Marlowe to repent of his atheism.

The following May, Thomas Kyd the dramatist was arrested on suspicion that he was concerned in writing certain seditious libels against the foreigners living in London. His papers were seized, and amongst them was found part of an heretical treatise denying the divine nature of Christ. This paper, Kyd declared, had been accidentally left by Marlowe in his papers some two years before.

On 18th May a warrant was issued to bring Marlowe before the Privy Council; he appeared on the 20th and was ordered to attend daily. Meanwhile inquiries were made; a certain Richard Baines produced a long list of charges against Marlowe in which he declared that 'He affirmeth that Moyses was but a Iugler, and that one Heriots being Sir W. Raleigh's man, can do more than he'. It was also stated that Marlowe had persuaded a certain Richard Cholmeley to become an atheist. An informer was set to watch Cholmeley, and reported that 'hee saieth & verely beleueth that one Marlowe is able to shewe more sounde reasons for Atheisme then any devine in

[1] *The Groatsworth of Witte.* Bodley Head Quartos, Vol. VI, p. 43.

Englande is able to geue to prove devinitie & that
Marlow tolde him that hee hath read the Atheist
lecture to Sr Walter Raliegh & others.'

After Marlowe's sudden death on 30th May,
Kyd wrote two letters to the Lord Keeper to
defend himself, in the first of which he says: 'ffor
more assurance that I was not of that vile opinion,
Lett it but please yor L^p to enquire of such as he
conversed wthall, that is (as I am geven to vnderstand) wth *Harriot*, *Warner*, *Royden* and some
stationers in Paules churchyard'. In the second
letter he repeats the charges against Marlowe and
adds, 'he [Marlowe] wold perswade wth men of
quallitie to goe vnto the k of *Scotts* whether I
heare Royden is gon and where if he had liud he
told me when I saw him last he meant to be.'[1]

In the summer of 1593, Sir Walter and his
brother, Carew Raleigh, supped with Sir George
Trenchard. Amongst those present were Sir
Ralph Horsey and the Rev. Ralph Ironside,

[1] Kyd's first letter, the heretical treatise, and the charges
against Marlowe, so far as they are printable, are to be
found in *The Works of Thomas Kyd*, edited by Dr. F. S.
Boas. The two papers dealing with Cholmeley are
printed in my *Shakespeare's Fellows*. Kyd's second letter
was reproduced in *The Times Literary Supplement* of
2nd June 1921 by Mr. Ford K. Brown.

minister of Winterbottom. The talk turned on religion and the life to come. Though the Raleighs were sceptical and scoffing, the parson sturdily maintained his end until a deadlock in the argument was reached, when 'Sir Walter wished that grace might be sayed'. Horsey had said little, but listened in scandalised amazement.

In March 1594 a commission, emanating from Her Majesty's Commissioners for Causes Ecclesiastical, was appointed to inquire into alleged heresies in the county of Dorsetshire. The commissioners were Lord Thomas Howard, Viscount Bindon, Sir Ralph Horsey, Chancellor Francis James, John Williams, and Francis Hawley. The Commission met at Cerne Abbas. The framing of the interrogatories which were to be put to the witnesses leaves little doubt that some one at Sir George Trenchard's table had sent a very full report to London. The depositions and the interrogatories are to be found amongst the Harleian Manuscripts at the British Museum (6849, ff. 183–190). A complete transcript will be found in Appendix III on pp. 255–271.

The Inquiry at Cerne must have caused considerable stir, both in Dorsetshire and London. Great noblemen were ruthless in their animosities, and the chance of impeaching Raleigh on a charge of heresy was not to be missed. But the Inquiry was disappointing, and no capital charge could be framed from the hearsay evidence of country parsons and churchwardens.

Raleigh's faults were obvious, and his atheism, his pride, and, above all, his fall offered ample opportunity for the wits in the pay of his enemies. But his enemies, notably Essex and Southampton, were open to attack in one direction—the morals of courtiers were notoriously loose.

AVISA'S SUITORS
(a) H. W.

To return to *Willobie His Avisa*. Of Avisa's suitors, the most interesting is the last—H. W., with his friend, W. S.

According to the poem, H. W. is young, 'If yeares I want, why I will stay,' (138: 7); a 'headlong youth', who has never been in love before (129: 12). At the head of Canto XLIV he is called *Henrico Willobego*, but it is clear that he is not 'Willobie', the author of the poem, because the episode ends with the words, 'H. W. Was now againe striken so dead, that hee hath not yet any farder assaid, nor I thinke euer will, and where he be aliue or dead I know not, and therfore I leaue him' (170: 21).

W. S. is a 'miserable comforter comforting his frend with an impossibilitie, eyther for that he now would secretly laugh at his frends folly, that had giuen occasion not long before vnto others to laugh at his owne, or because he would see whether an other could play his part better then himselfe, & in vewing a far off the course of this louing Comedy, he determined to see whether it would sort to a happier end for this new actor, then it did for the old player' (116: 14). To H. W.'s complaint that Avisa is obdurate, he offers the cynical answer:

'She is no Saynt, She is no Nonne,

I thinke in tyme she may be wonne.' (121: 11); and adds some practical directions in the art of love which are not dissimilar to the XIXth Sonnet in the *Passionate Pilgrim*.

Remembering that *Willobie His Avisa* treats of important persons, there is strong probability that H. W. is to be identified with Henry Wriothesley, Earl of Southampton, and W. S. with William Shakespeare.

Southampton was born on 6th October 1573.[1] His father had died just before his eighth birthday, and he had passed under the wardship of Lord Burleigh. In due course he went up to St.

[1] See *The Third Earl of Southampton*, by Mrs. C. C. Stopes.

John's College, Cambridge, and graduated as Master of Arts, 'per gratiam', on 6th June 1589. The next year Burleigh set about procuring a wife for his charge, and considered that the most suitable candidate was his own granddaughter, Lady Elizabeth Vere, daughter of the Earl of Oxford; she was then aged fifteen. Southampton, however, being much occupied with his friendship with the Earl of Essex, was in no hurry. Both noblemen took part in Queen Elizabeth's notable visit to Oxford in September 1592, and it is recorded that Southampton made a brilliant impression. Soon afterwards the plague broke out in London and raged with great violence for some eighteen months.

Little seems to be known of Southampton's movements during 1593 and the first half of 1594 — the period immediately preceding the publication of *Willobie His Avisa* — but it was during these months that his intimacy with Shakespeare began. *Venus and Adonis* was entered on 18th April 1593, and the dedication to Southampton reads:

RIGHT HONOURABLE,

I KNOW not how I shall offend in dedicating my unpolished lines to your lordship, nor how the world will censure me for choosing so strong a prop to support so weak a burden: only if your honour seem but pleased, I account myself highly praised, and vow to take advantage of all idle hours, till I have honoured you with some graver labour. But if the first heir of my invention prove deformed, I shall be sorry it had so noble a god-father, and never after ear so barren a land, for fear it yield me still so bad a harvest. I leave it to your honourable survey, and your honour to your heart's content; which I wish may always answer your own wish and the world's hopeful expectation.

Your honour's in all duty,

WILLIAM SHAKESPEARE.

Mrs. Stopes and others, in commenting on *Venus and Adonis*, have suggested that, in common with other Elizabethan poems, it has a secondary intention and is, in fact, with the first group of the *Sonnets*, a plea to Southampton to marry.

A year later, on 9th May 1594, *The Rape of Lucrece* was entered and is also dedicated to Southampton, but in very different terms:

THE love I dedicate to your lordship is without end; whereof this pamphlet, without beginning, is but a superfluous moiety. The warrant I have of your honourable disposition, not the worth of my untutored lines, makes it assured of acceptance. What I have done is yours; what I have to do is yours; being part in all I have, devoted yours. Were my worth greater, my duty would show greater; meantime, as it is, it is bound to your lordship, to whom I wish long life, still length-ened with all happiness.

Your lordship's in all duty,

WILLIAM SHAKESPEARE.

If *Venus and Adonis* has a hidden meaning, so perhaps has *Lucrece*. It is at least clear that in the interval between the publication of the two poems Shakespeare had received many marks of favour from Southampton.

Shakespeare had quite suddenly become well known. At the end of 1592, Greene's ill-natured comments in the *Groatsworth of Witte* on the 'vpstart Crow', answered by Chettle in *Kindharts Dreame*, had drawn attention to his 'facetious grace in writting'; but the publication of *Venus and Adonis* brought him wide renown—not, it must be admitted, amongst the most reputable class of readers.

Unfortunately, nothing definitely is known of the relationship of Southampton and Shakespeare, though Rowe, with some diffidence, asserts that 'my lord of *Southampton* at one time gave him a thousand pounds to go through with a purchase which he heard he had a mind to'. Assuming, as is probable, that most of the *Sonnets* were addressed to Southampton, the intimacy must have been extraordinarily close. If so, it would have caused unfavourable comment that so noble a youth should move in familiarity with a common player in interludes.[1]

A few stray facts are, however, worth mentioning. The first is the discovery (announced in *The Times Literary Supplement* of 17th September 1925, by Mrs. L. G. Thompson) that the curious name of Gobbo occurs in the Registers of Tichfield, Southampton's home. It is not without significance; for Shakespeare made bold with familiar names. There were Bardolphs and Fluellens at Stratford; an Orsino visited London in 1600; there was an Elephant in the South Suburbs, near the Globe; then there were the three louses; and Katharine Hamlet, whose drowning in the Avon is immortalized in Ophelia. The name proves nothing, but it suggests a link between Tichfield and *The Merchant of Venice*.

The second fact is that there should have been an edition of *Willobie His Avisa* in 1609; for in that year were published the *Sonnets* and the mysterious first quarto of *Troilus and Cressida*, both apparently obtained from improper sources.

[1] See *Sonnets*, xxxvi, ll. 9–13.

It will also be noticed that the correspondence between H. W. and Avisa is interspersed with Italian mottoes. In 1594 John Florio, afterwards the translator of Montaigne, was in Southampton's service.[1] Three years before this, Florio had published his *Giordino di Recreatione*, a collection of Italian proverbs; no less than seven of the Italian mottoes in *Willobie His Avisa* are to be found in Florio's book.

Meanwhile the Lady Elizabeth Vere was still waiting, but the Earl showed no enthusiasm. Amongst the Ladies-in-Waiting in need of a husband was the Lady Bridget Manners. The names of the Earl of Bedford and the Earl of Southampton were mentioned, but Lady Bridget said that if they were in her choice she 'would chouse my Lord of Wharton [a widower with five children] before them, for they be so yonge and fanastycall and would be so caryed away'.[2]

But Burleigh's patience was limited. In 1594 an eligible party appeared in the new Earl of Derby; the match was concluded and Southampton had to pay £5,000.[3]

---

[1] Stopes, p. 83.

[2] See *Queen Elizabeth's Maids of Honour*, by Violet A. Wilson, p. 193.

[3] Stopes, p. 86.

In identifying H. W. with Southampton, it is not absolutely necessary that he should have ever known the real Avisa; but it is quite possible that he was in Sherborne, for his brother-in-law, Sir Matthew Arundel, lived at Shaftesbury, the next stage on the Sherborne-London road.

(b) THE OTHER SUITORS

Before her marriage, Avisa was approached by a nobleman. He was elderly, wealthy, and of great estate. The only other clue to his identity—if it is a clue—is in the lines, 'Vnhappie Lillie loues a weed' (46 : 3), which suggests a coat of arms.

The next suitor is called 'Caveleiro'. He was a comparative stranger, but had seen her before (57: 19); he has 'wannie cheekes' and 'shaggie lockes' (61: 8). Fleay suggested Sir Ralph Horsey; taken with the lines in *Penelope's Complaint* and the name itself, the identification is probable.

There was evidently some scandal about Horsey at this time. John Harington, in his Apologie for *The Metamorphosis of Aiax* (1596), summons in defence a jury of his friends which includes: 'Ralph Horsey, knight, the best housekeeper in Dorsetshire, a good freeholder, a deputie Lieutenant. Oh Sir, you keep hauks, and hounds, and hunting horses; it may be some made fellow will say, you must stand in the Bath vp to the chinne for spending fiue, for spending fiue hundred poundes, to catch hares, and Partridges, that might be taken with fiue poundes.' In a sidenote is added, 'According to the tale in the hundred merry tales.'[1]

It is possible that Harington himself comes into the story of Avisa, for in 'The Victory of English Chastity', presumably added to the second edition of *Willobie His Avisa* in this same year 1596, 'Rogero' is called in to decide between the rival claims of Penelope and Avisa (246 : 21). Rogero is a prominent character in Ariosto's *Orlando Furioso*, which Harington had translated and published in a sumptuous folio in 1592. Rogero is a likely enough pseudonym for Harington.

———

'D. B.' has even less personality. He has recently inherited a farm 'Woorth fortie pounds, at yearely rent' (82 : 7), and Avisa suggests—

'You seeme as though you lately came
From London' (83 : 13).

———

Of 'D. H.' a little more is said. He is given the name of Didymus Harco; he is far from home, yet

———

[1] Signature Bb7ᵛ. It is very tempting to connect these expensive partridges with Avisa.

he has often 'seene the Western part'; he is lavish
of his gifts. After his first rebuff he renews the
attempt, but finding Avisa with her maids, he
goes home and sends her a ring with the posy:

'No frend to faith

That will remaine, till both our death'. (114:23)
Didymus suggests Thomas, and at a guess,
Harco might be Howard.

Lord Thomas Howard of Bindon sat with Sir
Ralph Horsey on the Commission at Cerne in
March 1594.

THE AUTHORSHIP OF
WILLOBIE HIS AVISA

The poem is introduced by Hadrian Dorrell,
who contributes an Epistle Dedicatory 'To all the
constant Ladies & Gentlewomen of England that
feare God', and an 'Epistle to the gentle &
courteous Reader'. In the latter he relates how
not long since 'my very good frend and chamber
fellow M. Henry Willobie, a yong man, and a
scholler of very good hope, being desirous to see
the fashions of other countries for a time, departed
voluntarily to her Maiesties seruice. Who at his
departure, chose me amongst the rest of his
frendes, vnto whome he reposed so much trust,

that he deliuered me the key of his study, and the
vse of all his bookes till his returne. Amongest
which (perusing them at leysure), I found many
prety & witty conceites, as I suppose of his owne
dooing' (5: 2). He then proceeds to discuss the
poem, leaving it in doubt whether it is to be taken
as fact or fiction.

Two years later, in 1596, the same Hadrian
Dorrell adds an 'Apologie', wherein he contra-
dicts himself by declaring that Avisa is a purely
fictitious person and that 'this poeticall fiction was
penned by the Author at least for thirtie and fiue
yeeres since, (as will be proued) and lay in wast
papers in his study, as many other prettie things
did, of his deuising; and so might yet haue continued still (as his *Susanna* yet doth) had not I,
contrarie to his knowledge, with paine collected
it' (238: 26).

Dorrell's word would seem, therefore, to be quite
unreliable. Moreover, the circumstances are
suspicious; for this discovery of papers left behind
in a study is not an uncommon literary device to
preserve anonymity or to give a touch of truth to
an improbable fiction. Lodge's *Rosalynde*, for
instance, is called 'Euphues Golden Legacie,
found after his death in his cell at Silexedra'. The
officious friend, too, who played pander for the

printer, was well known in the Elizabethan publishing trade.

After the Epistle come two poems in praise of *Willobie His Avisa*, signed by 'Abell Emet' and 'Contraria contrarijs Vigilantius : Dormitanus'. The real Vigilantius was a presbyter of the fourth century who wrote a book against superstitious practices, relic worship and the like. This roused the indignation of Jerome, who answered with his treatise, *Contra Vigilantium*, in which with heavy humour he calls his opponent 'Dormitantius'. It is not too far-fetched an explanation that 'Vigilantius Dormitanus' signifies 'one who refuses to accept popular beliefs'.

There is, of course, always the possibility that Willobie is a real person, and this was maintained by Sir Sidney Lee in the *Dictionary of National Biography*, which states that Willoughy 'was the second son of Henry Willoughby, a country gentleman of Wiltshire, by Jane, daughter of one Dauntsey of Lavington, Wiltshire. A younger brother was named Thomas . . . Henry matriculated as a commoner from St. John's College, Oxford, on 15 December 1591, at the age of sixteen . . . He may be the " Henry Willoughbie " who graduated B.A. from Exeter College on 28 February 1594-5'.

Mr. Charles Hughes, who supported this view in his edition of *Willobie His Avisa* (1904), added some further details and showed that on 10th December 1591, 'three young men entered their names at the University as follows:

> Henry Willobie, Wilts, arm. f. [*armigeri filius*] 16, St. John's.
>
> Thomas Darrell, Berks, cler. f. [*clerici filius*] Brasenose.
>
> William Marvyn, Wilts, gen. f. [*generosi filius*] Exeter.

That Willobie and Marvyn, the sons of two Wiltshire neighbours, were friends and companions is likely enough, and it is made more likely from the fact that Henry Willobie changed his college to Exeter, and that both young men took their B.A. degree on the same day, February 1594-95.'

Unfortunately, this fact somewhat upsets the theory of Henry Willoughby's authorship of *Willobie His Avisa* because, if the real Willoughby took his degree in the ordinary way in February 1595, it is not likely that he would have 'departed voluntarily on her Maiesties seruice' in 1594.

In the 1596 edition of *Willobie His Avisa* a new poem is added—*The Victory of English Chastity*—and is signed 'Thomas Willoby Frater Henrici

P

Willoby nuper defuncti'. But, both in metre and style, it bears every indication of being the work of the author of *Willobie His Avisa.*

Mr. Arthur Acheson declares that Matthew Roydon is the real author of *Willobie His Avisa.*

Though little is now known of the work of Roydon, he appears to have held a high reputation as a man of letters at this time. Nashe, in his address 'To the Gentlemen Students of Both Universities', prefaced to Greene's *Menaphon* (1589), says:

'Neither is he [Spenser] the onely swallow of our Summer, (although *Apollo*, if his Tripos were vp againe, would pronounce him his *Socrates*,) but being forborne, there are extant about London many most able men to reuiue Poetry, though it were executed tenne thousand times, as in *Platoes*, so in Puritans Common-wealth; as, namely, for example, *Mathew Roydon*, *Thomas Achlow*, and *George Peele*; the first of whom, as he hath shewed himselfe singular in the immortall Epitaph of his beloued *Astrophell*, besides many other most absolute Comike inuentions (made more publique by euery mans praise, then they can be by my speech), so the second hath more then once or twice manifested his deepe witted schollership in places of credite.'[1]

[1] McKerrow. iii. 323.

In 1594 Chapman dedicated his *The Shadow of Night* to his 'dear and most worthy friend, Master Matthew Roydon'. At this time, as the passages already quoted on p. 211 show, Roydon was one of Raleigh's group. In later years he was reduced to extreme poverty.

Mr. Acheson's claims for Roydon are far-reaching and cannot be accepted without further proofs. Three poems, however, are definitely known to be Roydon's work. The first is a short Ode prefixed to Thomas Watson's ΕΚΑΤΟΜΠΑΘΙΑ *or Passionate Centurie of Loue* (1581), which is signed and includes the lines:

'This fauour hath put life into my pen,
 That heere presentes his first fruite in this
  kinde.'

The second is printed before Sir George Peckham's *True Report* (1583). The third is *An Elegie, or friends pastorall, for his Astrophill*.[1] It is unsigned; but it is quoted several times as the work of Roydon in Robert Allott's *England's Parnassus* (1600).

Some of the stanzas of the elegy bear so close a resemblance to stanzas in *Willobie His Avisa* that there is strong probability that Mr. Acheson is right.

[1] Printed in *The Poetical Works of Edmund Spenser*. Edited by J. C. Smith and E. de Selingcourt, Oxford, p. 556.

In the opening canto of *Willobie His Avisa* the author says of himself:

> 'My sleepie Muse that wakes but now,
> Nor now had wak't if one had slept.'

The natural inference is that the author has not written verses for some time, but has been roused to answer an attack made by some other poet.

CONCLUSION

When so many of the pieces are missing it is clearly impossible to reconstruct the form of the original with any sense of assurance. Nevertheless, the fragments do seem to form a coherent pattern; and so, while fully conscious of the incompleteness of my proofs, I venture to summarise my conclusions:

i. *Willobie His Avisa* went into six editions before 1635; it was therefore a popular book.

ii. It was concerned with the private lives of great men and not with any hole-in-the-corner intrigue.

iii. Avisa, the heroine of the poem, lived in the neighbourhood of Cerne Abbas and Sherborne, but the interest of the story to its original readers was in her connection with certain of her illustrious neighbours.

iv. Throughout the book, the morals of courtiers in general are attacked. The writer, therefore, was not at the time attached to the Court or to anyone in favour at Court.

v. Amongst those attacked are the Earl of Southampton and his protégé, William Shakespeare. The author of *Willobie His Avisa* was therefore an enemy of the Essex-Southampton group.

vi. Sir Ralph Horsey, whom Sir Walter Raleigh had every reason to dislike, was also attacked.

vii. The evidence of style suggests that Matthew Roydon may have been the author. Roydon was one of Sir Walter Raleigh's personal followers.

viii. The poem was written as an answer to an attack made on the Raleigh group.

We may, perhaps, venture a little further to consider what this attack was. In the verses signed 'Vigilantius : Dormitanus' occur these lines:

> '*Yet* Tarquyne *pluckt his glistering grape,*
> *And* Shake-speare, *paints poore* Lucrece
> *rape.* . . .

> *Then* Aui-Susan *ioyne in one,*
> *Let* Lucres-Auis *be thy name,*
> *This* English Eagle *sores alone,*
> *And farre surmounts all others fame,*
> > *Where high or low, where great or small,*
> > *This* Brytan Bird *out-flies them all.'* (19 : 13)

It is evident that 'Vigilantius : Dormitanus' intends *Willobie His Avisa* to be coupled in the reader's mind with Shakespeare's *Lucrece.*

We have seen how often a secondary intention is to be found in the poems of the 1590's. The most important poem produced by the followers of Southampton in 1594 was *The Rape of Lucrece.* Shakespeare in all probability had no intention of making his Tarquin a portrait of any living person; but his readers, incurable in their search for hidden meanings, saw in this poem, written for the Essex-Southampton group, a very considerable likeness between Tarquin the Ravisher and their enemy, Raleigh the Proud. Raleigh, too, had sinned against chastity, and, like Tarquin, he seemed to have paid for his sin by everlasting banishment.

And so, in the summer of 1594, the followers of Sir Walter Raleigh, who were living with him at Sherborne, stung beyond endurance by these incessant attacks on their patron, composed this poem of *Willobie His Avisa*, seeking to hold his enemies up to ridicule, not in any fable culled from Antiquity, but with the plain tale of the country hostess who so triumphantly humiliated her noble wooers.

Willobie His Avisa is the sequel to Shakespeare's *Lucrece*.

APPENDIX I

Extracts from the preliminary matter of *Penelope's Complaint*.[1]

(a) Title-page

PENELOPE'S COMPLAINT / Or / *A Mirrour for wanton* / Minions / Taken out of Homer's Odissea / and written in English / Verse / *By Peter Colse* / *Armat spina rosas, mella tegunt apes* / (rule) / LONDON / Printed by *H. Jackson* dwelling in / Fleetstreet, and are to be sold at his / shop under Temple-barre / gate. 1596. /

(b) The Dedication

To the vertuous and chaste Ladie,
The Ladie Edith, wife of the right worship-
full Sir Rafe Horsey, knight, increase of all
honourable vertues.

PERUSING (vertuous Ladie) a Greeke Author, entituled Odyssea *(written by* Homer *prince of Greeke poets) noting therein, the chast life of the Ladie* Penelope *(in the twentie yeers absence of hir loving lord* Ulysses) *I counterfeited a discourse, in English verses, terming it her Complaint: which treatise comming to the view, of certaine of my special-friends, I was by them oftentimes encited to publish it. At length*

---

[1] As the unique copy of *Penelope's Complaint* is now in America, these extracts are taken from the late Mr. C. Hughes' edition of *Willobie His Avisa*.

weying with my selfe, the shipwracke that noble vertue chastitie is subject unto: and seeing an unknowne Author, hath of late published a pamphlet called Avisa *(over-slipping so many praiseworthy matrons) hath registred the meanest: I have presumed under your Ladiships patronage to commit this my* Penelopes *complaint (though unperfectly portraied) to the presse: not doubting but the Etimológie of so rare a subject, enchased with the Physiognomie of your excellent chastitie: so worthie a conclusion cannot but be a sufficient argument both to abolish* Venus *Idolaters, & also to counter-vaile the checkes of* Artizans *ill willers, which carpe at al, but correct nothing at al: measuring other mens labours, by their owne idle humors. Thus offering unto your Ladiship the firstlings of my scholers crop, for a satisfaction of my presumption, and hoping you wil pardon my boldnes, and accept of this my proffered service, I commit you to the grace and tuition of the Almightie.*

Your Ladiships to commaund

PETER COLSE.

(c) Verses by S. D.

Amico suo charissimo P. C. S. D.

QUID quærit titulos, quid dotes iactat Avisa.
    Anne ea Penelope est æquiparanda tuæ?
Penelope clara est, veneranda fidelis: Avisa
    obscura, obscuro fæmina nata loco.

Penelope satrapæ est conjux illustris: Avisa
conjux cauponis, filia pandochei.
Penelope casta est cum sponsus abesset: Avisa
casta suo sponso nocte diéque domi.

Penelopeia annos bis denos mansit: Avisa
tot (vix credo) dies intemerata foret.
Penelopeia procos centum neglexit: Avisa
Vix septem pretium sustinuitque precem,
Penelope nevit, pensum confecit: Avisa
lassauit nunquam pendula tela manus.
Penelope Graijs, Latijs celebratur: Avisa
unus homo laudes, nomen, & acta canit.
Ergo Penelope vigeat, cantetur: Avisa
nullo Penelope est æquivalenda modo.

(d) To the Reader

To the Reader.

HAVING taken upon me (Gentlemen) to pipe with *Hiparchion*, though my musicke be not melodious inough to content the proud *Thessalians*, yet I doubt not but poore shepheards will stirre their stumps after my minstrelsie, If the stranes be too harsh, to delight your stately eares (pardon me and accept my mind, and not my musicke) I stretch my strings as I can, desiring rather to teach the simple their uniforme cinque pace, then effect Courtiers in their lofty galliards, which alter every day with new devises. The cause I have contrived so pithie a matter in so plaine a stile, and short verse, is: for that a vaine-glorious *Avisa* (seeking by slaunder of her superiors, to eternize her folly) is in the like verse, (by an unknowen Authour) described: I follow (I say) the same stile, & verse, as neither misliking the methode, nor the matter, had it beene applyed to some worthier subject. Thus hoping you wil courteously accept my *Penelopes Complaint*, I wil shortly make you amends with her Will, and Testament, in Pentameters, wherein I wil stretch my wits to Ela, to shew my duetie, and satisfie your desires: and so farewell.

Peter Colse.

APPENDIX II

Additional matter appended to later editions of *Willobie His Avisa,* reprinted from the copy of the sixth edition, in the British Museum.

A.

THE

A P O L O G I E,

shewing the true meaning of

WILLOBIE his

AVISA.

TO a new Edition give me leave to adde a new Instruction, for such as I vnderstand, haue made of the other, a false and captious construction. If *Sapiens* come *à Sapore,* (as some will have it, and that as the Taste iudgeth of meates, so wise men iudge of natures and intents) I maruaile that some men so greatly affecting the name of wisedome, have by rash iudgement, (the badge of folly) shewed themselves so much vnwise, and without sap. But I see that as it happeneth in the distemperature of the body, so it often fareth in the disorders of the minde: for the body being oppressed with the venemous malice of some predominate humor, the seate of iudgement which is the taste, is corrupted: and meates, which of their owne nature are wholesome and sweete, seeme vnto the mouth (ill affected) / both bitter, vnsauorie, and vnwholesome: [123

So the heart being possessed with a veine of vanitie, or a spirit of preiudicate opinion, directeth iudgement by the line of fancie, not of reason: and the bitternesse of his owne infected folly, marres the sweete taste of other mens simple and honest meaning. Therefore because some haue applyed this Poeme, as they ought not; I am inforced to speake that which I thought not.

Many branches of errors, have sprouted forth from the roote of one fond and misconstrued conceite. The growing of such grafts, I hoped that I had sufficiently preuented in the Preface first printed with this booke. But this is the generall fault of all rash Readers, when they see a booke, they turne either to the middest, or the latter end or at all aduentures reading that which at first opening they happen on, if that presently doe not fit their fancie, they will sodainly pronounce a definitiue sentence of condemnation, both against the matter and the maker: as if by the inspiration of some Pythian Oracle, they were presently brought in possession of the whole sence, meaning and intent of the Author, having reade neither the preface, nor perchance six lines of the whole booke.

But most I marvaile that one P. C. (who seemeth to bee a Scholler) hath beene carried away with this streame of misconceiued folly: For I dare pawne my life, that there is no particular woman in the world, that was either partie or priuie to any one sentence or word in that booke. This poeticall fiction was penned by the Author at least / [124 for thirtie and fiue yeeres since, (as it will be proued) and lay in wast papers in his study, as many other prettie things did, of his deuising; and so might haue continued still (as his *Susanna* yet doth) had not I, contrarie to his knowledge, with paine collected it; and (in consideration of the good end, to which it was directed) published it. Seeing therefore that I gave the offence, I must satisfie for it, in defending innocents from slanderous tongues. This plaine Morall deuice was plotted only for the repression and opening of *Vice;* and to the exaltation and triumph of *Vertue*, as hee himselfe saith.

> *My sleepy Muse that wakes but now,*
> *To vertues prayse hath past her vow.*

Vertue therefore being *Genus*, and Chastitie *Species*, if hee should haue described it, either in *Genere* or *Specie*, as some haue done, he might haue beene as obscure as some others haue beene. Hee fained therefore an *Individuum*, as it were a particular of this speciall, the more familiarly to expresse it, as it were in common talke, as if one did answere another, to delight the reader the more, with variety of folly quenched presently, with the like varietie of Vertue. To this fained *Individuum*, he gave this fained name *Auisa*. Which poeticall fiction P. C. calleth a pamphlet. It is folly for a man to despise that which he cannot mend. The Author was vnknowne, not because hee could not; but because hee would not know him: his true name being open in euery Page. He saith: the Author hath registred the mea- / nest. I thought [125 that Chastitie had not beene the meanest, but rather one of the greatest gifts, that God giueth to men or women. If by the meanest, he meane any other obiect or subiect of *Willobie* his Muse, then Chastity itselfe (vnder the fained name of *Auisa*) it is a meaning of his owne making; and a subiect of his owne suggestion, far from the mind of the first maker. None can eternize their folly in things which they neuer thought of: but I pray God some other haue not eternized their follies, more wayes then one. If this fained name of *Auisa* mislike any man, for any hidden or priuate cause to the Author or me vnknowne, let him call it what he will: So that he vnderstand that it is Chastity it selfe, not any woman in the world, that is fained to give these foyles to this foule vice.

Therefore, whereas some in their grauity despise it for the lightnesse, and thinke it but a fantasticall toy, without any reach or secret sence, I will not striue to turne the course of that streame. Yet if my fancie might be admitted a iudge in this matter, it would produce a sentence of a farre contrary nature. For it seemeth rather to me that the Author intending some rare exploit, endeuoured to describe the doubtful combat, that is daily fought betweene Vice and Vertue, two princes of great power. And to that end he chose out two of the most approued Captaines of both the Campes to trie the quarrell. Out of the one hee tooke *Luxuriam*, Lecherie, which as we see, swayeth the minds of the greatest men, and commandeth largely. Out of the other, / he opposeth *Castitatem*, Chastitie, a [126 souldier rarely seene (in these dayes) to resist the enemies Push, and therefore in one of his verses, is called A Phœnix, or rare-seene bird.

The souldiers which hee drawes forth to fight vnder the

banner of this Captaine Lecherie, are all estates and degrees, and all Countries and Common-wealthes: meaning, that no men, from the highest estate to the lowest; no Countries, from the most ciuill to the most barbarous, are free from the seruile subiection of this raging principality: So that in this part, hee describeth the combats, the assaults, the intisements, and allurements, which Noblemen, Gentlemen, and all other loose and vnbridled mindes, can by money, wealth, pleasure, force, fancy, or any other patheticall passion, procure, or deuise, to raze the walls of besieged Chastity. Vnder whose banner he sendeth forth onely one poore woman, of a fayned name (minding to shew what the propertie of good women should bee) to resist so many, so mighty, so strong, and subtill enemies, fighting with such forcible weapons of honour authority, glorie, ease and pleasure. Surely, he imagined, that in some women there was yet left so much Chastitie, as was able to resist the lewd and diuelish temptations of all men whatsoeuer. And therefore, through the whole booke, he attributeth the victory to vertue, and the foyle to folly.

And farther, where as in other bookes, there is found a bare description onely, or naming of Vice or vertue, me thinkes in reading of this, my con- / ceite tels mee that [127 in the person of this woman all the morall vertues, with one voyce are heard pleading, and discoursing at large against vice, in a liuely action: In whose words, (if they bee considered from the beginning to the end) we may see, how the spirit of God striueth against the Spirit of Sathan,

Q

by reasons, by Scriptures, and by prophane Histories, to lay open the greatnesse, the foulenesse, the danger, and deceit of this deadly sin, that rageth so hotly, in the vnmortified members of mortall men.

On the other side me thinks I see how the Deuill calling together all his companie, in hope of a conquest tries all wayes and assayes all meanes to effect his desire. But his labor is imagined heere to be lost, and that there is some modesty, wisedome, honestie and feare of God remaining yet in some women, sufficient at all times to ouercome him. Therfore whosoeuer accounteth this Poeme, but a vaine fiction, cutteth the throate of all feminine faith, and robbeth all chast Ladies of their chiefest honour.

Some others, being much addicted to that sweete bitter sinne of Leacherie, thinke their secret practices of bauderie, to be too plainely described, and therefore labour to have it registred for a meere toy, I will not, as a Physition assay, with *Helleborus,* to purge their heads of those humors, least perhaps they bee of the men of *Abydus,* who (as *Aristotle* reporteth) being mad, tooke such delight in their madnesse that they were angry with them, that brought them to their wits. /   [128

Some others there be, who when they haue read this booke, have blushed to themselves, finding, as they thought, their very words and writings which they had vsed in the like attempts. In which is to be noted, the force of a guilty conscience, which feares where no feare is, and flyeth when no man followeth. These fancies (forsooth) have framed names to letters, of their owne deuices; and they have imagined places of their owne placing, so fitly for euerie description, that they will needs inforce the Author to speake of them, whom he neuer knew; to ayme at their fancies, whose faces he neuer saw; and to Cypher their names, whose natures to him were ignorant and strange.

Lastly; concerning the fained name of A VISA I haue shewed the Authors deuice, and his reason for the fiction, in the first Preface, which I thought would haue quailed all other fictions whatsoeuer.

But yet if farder yee will have my conceit, the order, words, and frame of the whole discourse, force me to think that which I am vnwilling to say. That this name in-sinuateth, that there was neuer such a woman seene, as heere is described. For the word A'VISA is compounded, (after the Greeke manner) of the priuatiue particle *A*, which signifieth *Non:* and of the participle *Visus, Visa, Visum*, which signifieth, Seene: So that *A'uisa* should signifie (by this) as much as *Non visa*, that is: Such a woman as was neuer seene. Which if it bee true, then *Auisa* is yet vnborne, that must reioyce in this prayse. The Author in this booke compareth this vertue of Chastity vnto a Bird, as is seene in / his introduction, saying: [129 *Of Vertues Bird*, my muse must sing.

For as the Birde by his wings mounteth in the aire vpwards to heauen: So Chastitie, where euer it is, makes the minde to mount from the base and filthy society of earthly conceits, and fits it to flie vp to God, in heauenly meditations; whereas lust and wicked pleasures, chaine the minde in thraldome of fleshly concupiscence (as *Prometheus* was tyed to the hill *Caucasus*) which will not suffer the thoughts to ascend by any meanes. The same Hieroglyphicall allusion they meant, that pictured S. *Iohn* with a Birde sitting by him, to signifie, that of all the foure Euangelistes, hee in his Gospell flew highest, and spake most of the Dietie of Christ. Now therefore the latine word of a Birde being *Auis*, and the Author (perchance) alluding vnto that, did the rather call his victorious mounting victory of Vertue, by the name of *Auisa*, as alluding to his owne allusion. If any man therefore by this, should take occasion to surmise, that the Author meant to note any woman, whose name sounds something like that name, it is too childish and too absurd, and not beseeming any deepe iudgement, considering there are many things, which cannot be applyed to any woman.

But to conclude, thus much, I dare precisely auouch, that the Author intended in this discourse, neither the description or prayse of any particular woman; nor the naming or cyphering of any particular man. But in generall vnder a fained name insinuateth what godly and constant women / should doe, and say in such lewde tempta- [130 tions. And also, vnder fained letters, generally expresseth, what course most of these lawlesse suters take, in pursuit of their fancied fooleries, and therefore this P. C. hath offred manifest iniurie to some, what euer they bee, whom his priuate fancie hath secretly framed in conceit.

This is the least that I could say, and the last that euer I wil say touching this matter in defence of my friend.

If any notwithstanding will continue the errour of their
vnsatisfied minds they must for euer rest in the rightlesse
erring, till the Authour (now of late gone to
God) returne from Heauen to satisfie them
farder touching his meaning. And so
farwel. Oxford this 30. of *June*.

1569.

* *
*

Thine to vse,

Hadrian Dorrell. | [131

B.

The victorie of English Chastitie,
Vnder the fained name of
AVISA

FOr beauties Ball, in *Ida*-Vale,
  Three Nimphes at once, did once contend,
The Princely *Shepheard* of the *Dale*,
By iudgement did the quarrell end:
    That *Paris* might faire *Hellen* haue,
    The *Golden Price* to *Venus* gave.

In *Sea-bred* soyle, on *Tempe* downes,
Whose siluer spring, from *Neptunes* Well,
With mirth salutes the neighbour townes,
A hot *Contention* lately fell:
  Twice two sweet *Graces*, vrge the strife,
  Of two which was the *Constant'st* wife

Faire *Venus* vaunts *Penelops* fame
From *Greece*, from listes of *Lauin Land*
Proud *Iuno* stoutly doth the same,
Whose prayse in princely wealth doth stand:
  They both condemne *Diana's* choyce,
  That to *Auisa* gave her voyce. /   [133

Then came the pale *Athenian Muse*,
Whose learned wisdome past them all,
She with *Diana* did refuse
The *Grecians* prayse: though *Iuno* call,
  Chaste *Wit* to *Wealth* here will not yeeld:
  Nor yet to strangers leaue the field:

Conten-
tion

A noble-
man of
Greece,
not farre
from He-
licon.

Whil'st *Eris* flasht these fretting flames,
A Noble prince in *Rosie* borne,
Rogero hight, to *Angry* dames,
His flying steed, and pace did turne,
  Which done they all pid straight agree,
  That this *Rogero*, Iudge should be.

On flowrie bancks, this Councell pla'st,
From iealous *Iuno's* enuious eyes,
Long smothered hate flames forth at last,
In furious smoakes of angry cries:
    As though she had the Garland wan,
    With scoffing termes, she thus began.

Stoop *Grecian* trumpes, cease *Romans* prayse,   "
Shut vp with shame, your famous dames;   "
Sith we our selues *Base Britans* rayse   "
To ouer-Top their chiefest fames: "
    With *Noble* faith what madnesse dare.   "
    Such *Nouell* guestes and faith compare? "

the Oration of Iuno against English Chastity vnder the name, of Auisa.

Penelope must now contend   "
For chaste renowne: whose constant heart, "
Both Greeks and Latines all commend   "
With poore *Auisa* new vpstart;   "
    I scorne to speake much in this case, "
    Her prayses *Riuall* is so base. /   "
                          [134

Penelope sprang from Noble house,   "
By Noble match, twice Noble made,   "
Auisa, both by Syre and spouse,   "
Was linckt to men of meanest trade: "
    What furie forc't *Diana's* wit,   "
    To match these two so farre vnfit?   "

,, The *Grecian* dame of princely peeres
,, Twice fifty flatly did denie;
,, Twice ten yeeres long in doubtfull feares,
,, Could new *Auisa* so reply?
,, And she that is so stout and strong,
,, Could she have staid but halfe so long?

,, Fie, leaue for shame, thus to commend,
,, So base a *Britaine*, shall I speake?
,, I think these Muses did intend,
,, To blow a glasse that should not breake:
,, Here *Venus* smilde, and *Iuno* staid,
,, Iudge now (quoth she) for I haue said.

When *Pallas* heard this rufling rage,
These toying iestes, this false surmise:
Shee paws'd which way she might asswage,
The flame that thus began to rise,
  With setled grace and modest eye,
  Thus did shee frame her milde reply.

The reply
of *Pallas*
against
Iuno in
defence of
Auisa.

,, Thou princely *Iudge* here maist thou see,
,, What force in *Error* doth remaine,
,, In Enuious Pride what fruites there be,
,, To writhe the paths, that lie so plaine:
,, A double darknes drownes the mind,
,, Whom selfe will make so wilfull blind, / [135

Can *Britaine* breede no *Phœnix* bird,   ,,
No constant feme in English field?   ,,
To Greece to Rome, is there no third,   ,,
Hath *Albion* none that will not yeeld?   ,,
    If this affirme you will not dare,   ,,
    Then let me *Faith* with *Faith* compare.   ,,

Let choyce respect of *Persons* slide,   ,,
Let *Faith and Faith* a while contend,   ,, *Willoby*
Vrge not the *Names* till cause be tride,   ,, described
'Tis onely *Faith*, that we commend,   ,, no parti-
    We striue not for *Auisa's* fame,   cular
    We recke not of *Auisa's* name.   ,, woman,
                                          ,, but only
                                            Chastity
                                            and faith
                                            her selfe
To proue him vaine, that vainely striues,   ,, under the
That Chastity is no where found,   ,, name of
In English earth, in British wiues,   ,, *Auisa.*
That all are fickle, all vnsound,   ,,
    We framde a wench, we fain'd a name,   ,,
    That should confound them all with shame. ,,

To this at first you did consent,   ,,
And lent with ioy a helping hand,   ,,
You both at first were well content,   ,, Chastity
This fained frame should firmely stand,   ,, is named
    We to *Diana* gaue the maide,   ,, Avisa,
    That she might no way be betraid.   ,, *quasi ab*
                                            Aue ti
                                          ,, *volanto.*[1]

---

[1] The sidenotes have been somewhat shaved by the binder.

” The mounting *Phœnix, chast desire,*
” This *Vertue* fram'd, to conquer *Vice,*
” This *Not-seene Nimph,* this heatlesse fire,
” This *Chast-found Bird,* of noble price,
”   Was nam'de *Auisa* by decree,
”   That *Name and nature* might agree. /   [136

„ If this *Avisa* represent,
„ *Chast Vertue* in a fained *name,*
„ If *Chastity* it selfe be ment,
„ To be extold with lasting fame:
„   Her Greekish gemme can *Iuno* dare,
„   With this *Auisa* to compare?

Chastity
is the gift
of God.

„ Let wise *Vlysses* constant mate,
„ Vaunt noble birth her richest boast,
„ Yet will her challenge come too late,
„ When *Pride and wealth* haue done their most
„   For this *Auisa* from aboue
„   Came downe whose Syre, is mighty *Ioue.*

„ How can you terme her then *Obscure,*
„ That shines so bright in euery eye?
„ How is she base that can endure,
„ So long, so much and mounts so hie?
„   If she you meane, haue no such power,
„   Tis your *Auisa,* none of our.

This not seene bird, though rarely found   „   True
In proud attire, in gorgeous gownes,   Chastity
                                                   is sooner
Though she loue most the countrie ground,   „   and
                                                   oftener
And shunnes the great and wealthy townes,   „   found in
                                                   the
       Yet if you know a bird so base,   „   poorest
       In this *Deuice* she hath no place.   „   then in
                                                   the
                                                   richest.

Was Greekish dame twice ten yeares chast,   „   Chastity
Did she twice fiftie flat deny?   daily
                                                   assaulted
Auisa hath *Ten thousand* past,   „   a thou-
                                                   sand
To thousands daily doth reply,   „   wayes yet
       If your *Auisa* have a blot   „   it still
                                                   getteth
       Your owne it is, we know her not. / [137   „   the
                                                   victorie.

Some greatly doubt your *Grecian* dame   „
Where all be true that Poets faine: „
But *Chastity* who can for shame,   „
Denie she hath, and will remaine.   „
       Though women daily doe relent.   „
       Yet this *Auisa* cannot faint.   „

She quels by *Reason* filthy *lust*,   „   The
Shee chokes by *Wisdome* leude Desires,   „   effects of
                                                   true
Shee shunnes the baite that Fondlings trust,   „   Chastitite
From Sathan's sleights she quite retires,   „
       Then let *Auisa's* prayse bee spread,   „
       When rich and poore, when all are dead."

,, Let idle vaine, and *Flewent Rigges*,

,, Be *Canton'de* with eternall shame,

,, Let blowing buddes of blessed twigges,

,, Let *Chaste-Auisa* liue with fame:

,,   This said, *Sweet Pallas* takes her rest,

,,   Iudge *Prince* (quoth she) what you thinke best.

The sentence of *Rogero* against *Iuno*.

But wise *Rogero* pawsing staid,

Whose silence seem'd to shew some doubt,

Yet this at last he grauely said:

Ye *Nimphes* that are so faire, so stout,

       Sith I your *Iudge* to Iudge must be,

       Accept in worth, this short decree.

,, The question is, where *Grecian Ghost*,

,, Can staine the stemme of *Troyan* rase:

,, Where *Ithac Nimphes* may onely boast,

,, And *Brittish Faith* account as base,

,,   Where old *Penelops* doubtfull fame,

,,   *Selfe Chastity* may put to shame? /   [138

,, I count *Ulysses* happy *Then*,

,, I deeme our selues as happy *Now*,

,, His wife denide all other men,

,, I know them yet that will not bow,

,,   For *Chastity* I durst compare,

,,   With *Greece*, with *Rome*, with who that dare

Our English earth such *Angels* breeds,   " England
As can disdaine all *Forraine* prayse,   " for Chastitie
For *Learning, Wit*, for *sober Deeds*,   " may yet
All *Europe Dames* may learne their wayes: " compare with any
    Sith I of both may take my choyce,   " country in the
    Our *Not-seene Bird* shall haue my voyce.   " world.

Sweete Chastity shall haue my hand,   "
In England found, though rarely seene,   "
Rare Chastitie, To this I stand,   "
Is still as firme, as erst hath beene: "
    While this *Auisa* is the shee,   "
    This *Chaste desire* shall *Victor* be.   " Conclusion

The *Rose* appeares in *Venus* face,
Vermillion dies pale *Iuno's* cheekes,
They both doe blush at this disgrace,
But *Iuno* chiefe, something mislikes,
    As though she felt some inward touch,
    That for her *Greeke* had spoke so much.

FINIS.

Thomas Willoby Frater
Henrici Willoby nu-
      per defuncti. / [139

APPENDIX III

Depositions of witnesses who gave evidence before the Commission held at Cerne Abbas on 21st March, 1594. (British Museum, Harleian MSS. 6849, ff. 183–190.) Names in SMALL CAPITALS are signatures. The depositions up to the end of p. 270 are in the writing of the Rev. Ralph Ironside.

Interrogatories to be ministred vnto such as ar to be examined in her ma^{tes} name by vertue of her heighnes Comission for cawses Ecclesiasticall.

1. Inp^{r}mis whome doe you knowe, or have harde to be susspected of Atheisme; or Apostacye? And in what manner doe you knowe or have harde the same? And what other notice can you geive therof?

2. Itm whome doe you knowe, or have harde, that have argued, or spoken againste? or as doubtinge, the beinge of anye God? Or what or where God is? Or to sweare by god, addinge if there be a god, or such like; and when and where was the same? And what other notice can you geive of anye such offend^{r}?

3. Itm whome doe you knowe or have harde that hath spoken against god his providence ouer the worlde? or of the worldes beginninge or endinge? or of p^{r}destinacion? or of heaven or of hell? or of the Resurreccion in doubtfull or contenciouse manner? when & where was the same? And what other notice can you geive of anye such offend^{r}?

4. Itm whome doe you knowe or have harde that hath spoken againste the truth of god his holye worde revealed to vs in the scriptures of the oulde & newe testament? or of some places therof? or have sayde those scriptures ar not to be beleieved & defended by her ma^tie for doctrine, & faith, and salvacion, but onlye of policye, or Civell gouernment, and when & where was the same? And what other notice can you geive of anye such offend^r?

5. Itm whome doe you knowe or have harde hath blasphemouslye cursed god: as in sayinge one time (as it rayned when he was a hawkinge) if there be a god A poxe on that god wch sendeth such weather to marr our sporte? or such like. Or doe you knowe or have harde of anye that hath broken froth into anye other wordes of blasphemye and when & where was the same? / [f. 183

6. Itm whome doe you knowe or have harde to have sayde, when he was dead his soule shoulde be hanged on the topp of a poale, and ronne god, ronne devill, and fetch it that woulde have it, or to like effecte? or that hath otherwise spoken againste the beinge; or imortallitye of the soule of man? or that a mans soule shoulde dye & become like the soule of a beaste, or such like; and when & where was the same?

7. Itm whome doe you knowe or have harde hath Counselled, procuered, ayded, Comforted, or conferred wth anye such offendo^r? when where & in what manner was the same?

8. Itm doe you knowe or have harde of anye of those
   offend^rs to affirme, all those that were not of there
   opinions towchinge the p^rmisses to be schismatickes,
   and in error? And whome doe you knowe hath soe
   affirmed? And when & where was it spoken?

9. Itm what can you saye more of anye of the p^rmisses?
   or whome have you knowne or harde can geive anye
   notice of the same? And speake all yor knowledge
   therin. /   [f. 183 *b*

Examiacions taken at Cearne in the Counte of
Dorset the XXIth daye of March in the
XXXVIth yeare of the raigne of o^r soueraigne
Ladye Queene Elizabeth &c. Before vs
Thomas Lorde Howard Vicount Howarde of
Bindon. Sr Raulfe Horsey knight ffraunces
James Chauncellor, John Willyams, & ffraunces
Hawley Esquiers by vertue of a Commission to
vs & others directed from some of her ma^tes
heigh Commissioners in Cawses Ecclesiasticall
&c.

John Hancocke parson of South Parrott sworne &
examined the daye & time above written. To the first
Interrogatory sayeth, that he remembereth noe man
susspected of Atheisme or Apostacye. And soe to the
reste of the Interrogatory he sayeth he can saye nothinge.

R

Richard Bryage churchwarden of South Parrott sworne & examined the daye above written; To the first Interrogatory this depon^t can saye nothinge. And soe he aunswereth to the rest of the Interrogatories.

John Jesopp minister of Gillinghame sworne & examined To the first Interrogatory he can saye nothinge of his owne knowledge; but he hath harde that one Herryott of Sr Walter Rawleigh his howse hath brought the godhedd in question, and the whole course of the scriptures but of whome he soe harde it he doth not remember. He alsoe further sayeth That he harde his brother doctor Jesopp saye; That Mr Carewe Rawley reasoninge wth Mr Parrye and Mr Archdeacon aboute the godhedd (as he coniectureth) his sayde brother thinckinge that Mr Archdeacon and Mr Parrye woulde take offence at that argum^t desiered the Lo: bushopp of Worchester (then beinge there) that he might argue wth the sayde Mr Rawleigh; for sayed he yor Lo^p shall heare him argue as like a pagan as eu*er* you harde anye. but the matter was soe shutt up, as this exa^t harde his sayde brother saye, & proceaded not to argum^t And further he saieth That he hath hard one Allen nowe of Portland Castle susspected of Atheisme, but of whome he harde it he remembereth not. /   [f. 184

To the rest of the Interrogatories he can remember noe more then he hath sayde before.

William Hussey Churchwarden of Gillingham sworne &

examined. To the first Inter*ogatory* sayeth that he hath harde Sr Walter Rawleigh susspected of Atheisme.

To the rest of the Inter*ogatories* he can saye nothinge.

John Davis Curate of motcombe sworne & exami*n*ed the daye and yeare abovesayde. To the first Inter*ogatory* sayeth that he knoweth of noe such parson directlye, but he hath harde Sr Walter Rawleigh by generall reporte hath had some reasoninge against the diet*y*e of god, and his omnipotencye. And hath harde the like of Mr Carewe Rawleigh, but not soe directlye. Alsoe he sayeth he harde the like report of one Mr Thinn of Wilsheire, wch he harde from a Barber in Warmister dwellinge in a bye Lane there, whoe toulde this depon^t he did marvell that a gent-*leman* of his credite shoulde deliu*er* worde to soe meane a man as him selfe tendinge to this sence as though god*es* pr*o*vidence did not reach ou*er* all creatures or to like effecte.

To the 2. 3. 4 & 5th Inter*ogatories* he sayeth noe more then as before is sayed. And to the 6th Inter*ogatory* he sayeth he hath harde that Sr Walter Rawleigh hath argued wth one Mr Ironsyde at Sr George Trenchard*es* towchinge the beinge, or imortallitye of the soule, or such like; but the c*e*rtaintye therof he cannot saye further, savinge askinge the same of Mr Ironsyde vppon the reporte aforesayde, he hath aunswered that the matter was not as the voice of the Countree reported therof, or to the like effecte. And to the rest of the Inter*ogatories* he can*not* saye more. / [f. 184*b*

Nicholas Jefferys pa*r*son of Weeke Reg*es* sworne & exami*n*ed the daye and yere above sayde.

1   To the first Inter*ogatory* this depon[t] sayeth that he doth
not knowe of his owne knowledge anye Atheist*es* w[th]in
the Countie of Dors*et* or plac*es* neare adioyninge: but he
hard by reporte of divers that S[r] Walter Rawleigh and his
retenewe ar gen*e*rallye susspected of Atheisme; and
especially one Allen of Portland Castle Leiftenant, And
that he is greate blasphem*er* & leight esteem*er* of Religion;
and therabout*es* cometh not to Devine s*er*vice or sermons.

3   To the 3 he sayeth he hath harde that one Herriott
attendant on S[r] Walter Rawleigh hath ben convented
before the Lord*es* of the Counsell for denyinge the
resurrecc*i*on of the bodye.

To the 6 he saieth That M[r] Ironsyde reported that he
was p[r]sent at S[r] George Trenchard*es* at the table when as
there were some speches of M[r] Carewe Rawleigh gentlye
reproved by S[r] Raulfe Horsey, whervnto he replied that he
had in deade sinned in manye thing*es* but what hurte had
come vnto him for it? Wherunto was aunswered al-
thougth there were noe hurte vnto his bodye yet there was
vnto his soule. the soule sayde M[r] Carewe Rawleigh what
is that? Whervppon M[r] Ironsyde was willed to deliu*er* his
opinion therof. whoe aunswered that it was a matter rather
to be beleeved, then to be disputed of. Then sayed S[r]
Walter Rawleigh, yet I praye you for o[r] Learninge Let vs
knowe. M[r] Ironsyde aunswered that it was, Actus primus
corporis organici vitam habens in potestate. And accordinge
to Devines it was the imortall substaunce created by god to
gou*er*ne this liffe, and after this liffe either to suffer
punishem[t], or receave ioye togeather wth the bodye

foreu*er*. It was againe demaunded what that actus primus
or im*m*ortall substance was? and he againe aunswered it was
the soule. It was obiected that was noe sufficient aunswer
nor like a scholler; but he annswered they were principua,
and therfore coulde goe noe heigher: for definicio &
definitum must convenire. And if it were demaunded
what a man was, it were a sufficient aunswer to saye he
were animall racionale; if you demande what animall
racionale was, the aunswere were sufficient to saye he was
a man or to like effecte. but he remembereth noe further
reporte made vnto him by the sayde Mr Ironsyde. / [f.185

To the 6th Inter*ogatory* this depon^t sayeth That aboute
some three yeres paste cominge to Blandforde out of
Hampsheire his horse was stayed & taken for a poste horse
by Sr Walter Rawleigh & Mr Carewe Rawleigh; where
this depon^t entreatinge to have his horse released for that
he was to ride home vnto his charge (from whence he had
ben*e* some tyme absent) to preach the nexte daye beinge
sundaye, whervnto Mr Carewe Rawleigh replyed, that he
this depon^t might goe home where he woulde; but his
horse shoulde preach before him. or to that effecte. And
more he cannot nowe call to rememberance of the
Inter*rogatories*.

Will*i*am Arnolde Vicker of Blandforde sworne and
exami*n*ed the daye & yere abovesaide.

To the first Inter*ogatory* this depon^t saieth that of his
owne knowledge he knoweth not anye man that hath
either in earnest or in sporte, or in waye of argum^t, either

denyed that there is a god or any parte or parcell of the scriptures. ffor heare saye he can saye nothinge; but Mr Ironsyde deliuered some speach vnto him concerninge some disputacion had betwene him & Mr Carewe Rawleigh concerninge the beinge or substance of the soule. And yet he remembereth he harde Mr Carewe Rawleigh saye at Gillingham there was a god in nature. And more he remembereth not. And further he sayeth he harde by an vncertain reporte of some strange opinions that shoulde be defended by Sr Walter Rawleigh, but wheither the same be true or not certainelye he knoweth not, or whoe they were that reported the same.

To the reste of the Interogatories he can saye nothinge. /

[f. 185b

Thomas Norman of Wayemouth Melcombe Reges minister sworne & examined the daye & yere abovesayde.

To the first Interogatory he this depon^t sayeth that of his owne knowlege he can saye nothinge; but he harde Mr Joanes saye that he & one Mr Rogers beinge in Companye wth one Allen of Portland Castle Leiftenant, woulde have sent for this depon^t to dispute of some matters; But Mr Joanes sayde he thought that this depon^t woulde not abyde reasoninge. And the sayde Allen sayde he woulde make many such ministers as this depon^t is verye fooles or to like effecte, as Mr Joanes sayde. Alsoe this depon^t harde the sayde Mr Joanes sonne saye that the sayde Allen did teare twoe Leaves out of a Bible to drye Tobacco on. And the sayd Mr Joanes sonne sayd, that the sayde Allen spake as if he denyed the immortallity of the

soule. Alsoe he sayeth that he harde of one Herryott of
Sr Walter Rawleigh his howse to be susspected of Atheisme.

To the rest of the Interogatories he can saye nothinge.

John Dench Churchwarden of Weeke Reges sworne &
examined &c.

To the 6th Interogatory this depon^t sayeth that he hath
harde one Allen Leiftennant of Portland Castle when he
was like to dye, beinge perswaded to make himselfe reddye
to God for his soule, to aunswer that he woulde carrye his
soule vp to the topp of an hill, and runne god, ruñe devill,
fetch it that will have it. or to that effecte. but whoe toulde
this Depon^t of it he remembereth not.

To the rest of the Interogatories he can saye nothinge. /

[f. 186

ffraunces Scarlett minister of Sherborne sworne &
examined &c.

To the first Interogatory he sayeth That one Olliuer
servant to Thomas Allen should saye that Mr Tillye the
preacher did deliuer diuers thinges in his sermon wch were
not true, for wheras he spake manye thinges of Moyses in
his Commendacion, he affirmed that Moyses was noe such
man, for he the sayde Moyses had lij whores. wch wordes
he spake to Mrs Elizabeth Whetcombe & Mrs Brewer as
they came togeither from the said Mr Tyllies sermon from
Lillington. At wch time he deliuered vnto them manye
other thinges in derogacion of God & the scriptures. and of
the immortallitye of the soule. Where at the sayd women
(as they toulde this depon^t) sayde that there eares did

this
relacion
of m^r
Scarlet
grounded
vpon y^e
report of

2 women
and one
Robt
Hyde is
denyed
by their
oath &
founde
otherwise
as apper-
eth by
their par-
ticuler
ex.
taken by
Sr Raufe
Horsey
& Doctor
James.

glowe, and that they neuer harde such mounsterous speches from anye man. And he further sayeth that a little before Christmas one Robte Hyde of Sherborne shomaker seinge this depon^t passinge by his doore, called to him & desyered to have some conference wth him. and after some speches, he entered into these speches.   Mr Scarlet you have preachett vnto vs that there is a god, a heaven & a hell, & a resurreccion after this Liffe, and that we shall geive an accompte of o^r worckes, and that the soule is immortall; but nowe sayeth he here is a companye aboute this towne that saye, that hell is noe other but povertie & penurye in this worlde; and heaven is noe other but to be ritch, and enioye pleasueres; and that we dye like beastes, and when we ar gonne there is noe more rememberance of vs &c. and such like.   But this Examin^t did neither then demande whome they were; neither did he deliuer any particulers vnto him And further saieth That it is generally reported by almost euery bodye in Sherborne, that the sayd Allen & his man aforesayde ar Atheistes.   And alsoe he sayeth there is one Lodge a shomaker in Sherborne accompted an Atheiste. /

To the 6th Interogatory he sayeth that he harde [f. 186b Mr Coxe or Randell of Sherborne (as he remembereth) saye that Allen sayde when he was a hawkinge, and that it rayned; That if god were in the bushe there he woulde pull him out wth his teeth or to the like effecte.

To the rest of the Interogatories he can saye nothinge.

Robte Asheborne of Sherborne Churchwarden sworne & examined

To the first Interogatory he sayeth nothinge of his owne

certaine knowledge, but sayeth that he hath harde report*es,* that a man of Thom*as* Allens, whose name he knoweth not cominge from Lyllington with certaine women of Sherborne, spake certaine word*es* in derogac*i*on of moyses, that he had manye whores and other speches to the like derogac*i*on of moyses and the scriptures.

To the rest of the Inter*ogatories* he can saye nothinge. /
[f. 187

Raphe Ironside Minister of Winterbor sworne & examin*ed* &c.—

To the first Inter*ogatory* he sayeth that for his owne knowledge he will aunswer; but for that he hath harde, & knoweth no aucthore to iustefye the same he is p*er*swaded by Counsell, that he is in daunger to be punished, and therfore refuseth to saye any thinge vppon uncertaine reporte vnlesse he coulde bringe in his auchore in p*ar*ticuler.

> The relac*i*on of the disputac*i*on had at S*r* George Trenchard*es* table betwene S*r* Walter Rawleigh, M*r* Carewe Rawleigh & M*r* Ironside herafter followeth, written by himselfe & deliu*er*ed to the Com*m*issioners vppon his oath.

Wednesdaye sevenight before the Assises sumer Laste I came to S*r* George Trenchard*es* in the afternone accompayned w*th* a fellowe minister, & frinde of myne m*r* Whittle Viccar of fforthington. There were then w*th* the Knight, S*r* Walter Rawleigh, S*r* Raulfe Horsey M*r* Carewe Rawleigh M*r* John ffitziames, &c. / Toward*es* the end of supper some loose speeches of M.r Carewe Rawleighes beinge gentlye reproved by S.r Raulfe Horsey in these wordes Colloquia prava corrumpunt bones mores. / M.r Rawleigh demaundes of me, what daunger he might incurr by such speeches? whervnto I aunswered, the wages of sinn is death. and he makinge leight of death as beinge common to all sinner & reightuous; I inferred further, that as that liffe w.ch is the gifte of god through Jesus Christ, is liffe eternall: soe that death w.ch is properlye the wages of sinne, is death eternall, both of the bodye, and of the soule alsoe. Soule quoth M.r Carewe Rawleigh, what is that? better it were (sayed I) that we would be carefull howe the Soules might be saved, then to be curiouse in findinge out ther essence. And soe keepinge silence S.r Walter requestes me, that for there instruccion I woulde aunswer to the question that before by his brother / was proposed vnto me. I have [f. 187b benn (sayeth he) a scholler some tyme in Oxeforde, I have aunswered vnder a Bacheler of Arte, & had taulke w.th diuines, yet heithervnto in this pointe (to witt what the reasonable soule of man is) have I not by anye benne re-solved. They tell us it is primus motor the first mover in a man &c. vnto this, after I had replied that howesoeuer the soule were fons et principuum, the fountaine, beginninge and cawse of motion in vs, yet the first mover was the braine, or harte. I was againe vrged to showe my opinion and hearinge S.r Walter Rawleigh tell of his dispute & scholler-shipp some time in Oxeforde I cited the generall definicion of Anima out of Aristotle 2° de Anima cap: 1°, & thence a subiecto proprio duduced the speciall definicion of the soule reasonable, that it was Actus primus corporis organici *ani*mantis humani vitam ha*b*entis in po*tenti*a: It was misliked of Sr Walter as obscure, & intricate: And I wth all yealded that though it coulde not vnto him, as beinge lerned, yet it must seme obscure to the most p^{r}sent, and therfore had rather saye wth devines plainly that the reasonable soule is a sperituall & im*m*ortall substance breathed into man by god, wherby he lyves & moves & vnderstandeth, & soe is distingushed from other Creatures; yea but what is that sperituall & im*m*ortall substance breathed into man &c. saieth Sr Walter; the soule q*uoth* I., naye then saieth he you aunswer not like a scholler. herevppon I endevoured to prove that it was schollerlike, naye in such disputes as these, vsuall, & necessarye to runne in circulum p*a*rtlye because def*inic*io rei was primum et imediatum principuum, and seinge primo non est prius, a man must of necessetie come backwarde & p*a*rtelye becawse def*inic*io & definitum be nature recip*r*oce the one conv*er*tiblie aunsweringe vnto the question made vppon the other. As for example, if one aske what is a man? you will saye he is a creature reasonable & mortall; but if you aske againe. what is a creature reasonable & mortall, you must of force come b*a*ckewarde, and aunswer, it is a man. et sic de ceteris. / . but we have principles in our mathematickes sayeth Sr Walter, as totum est minus quaml*i*b*et* sua p*a*rte. and aske me of it, and I can showe it in the table in the window in a man the whole beinge bigger then the p*a*rtes of it. I replied first that he showed quod est, not, quid est, that it was but not what it was; secondlye, that such demonstrac*i*on as y^t was

against the nature of a mans / soule beinge a sperite. [f. 188
for as his thing*es* beinge sensible were subiecte to the
sence; soe mans soule beinge insensible was to be discerned
by the sperite. nothinge more c*er*taine in the worlde then
that there is a god, yet beinge a sperite to subiecte him to
the sence otherwise then p*er*fected it is impossible. Marrye
q*uoth* S[r] Walter these 2 be like for neither coulde I lerne
heitherto what god is; M[r] ffitziames aunsweringe that
Aristotle shoulde saye he was Ens, Encium. I aunswered
that whether Aristotle dyinge in a feaver shoulde crie ens
encium miserere mei, or drowninge him selfe in Euripum
shoulde saye quia ego te non capio tu me capies, it was
vnc*er*taine, but that god was ens entium a thinge of thinge
havinge beinge of him selfe, & geivinge beinge to all
creatures, it was most c*er*taine, and confirmed by god him
selfe vnto moyses. yea but what is this ens entium sayeth
S[r] Walter? I aunswered it is God. And beinge disliked
as before S[r] Walter wished that grace might be sayed; for
that q*uoth* he is better then this disputac*i*on. Thus supp*er*
ended & grace sayed, I dep*ar*ted to Dorchester w[t] my
fellowe minister, and this to my rememberance is the
substance of that speach w[ch] S[r] Walter Rawleigh & I had
at Wolveton.

RAPHE IRONSIDE.

Theis ex[ons] before written are the trewe Copies
taken at Cern*e* the XXIth of March 1593
before the Lo: Viscount Bindon S[r] Raufe

Horsey Knight, M·r· Doecto·r· James Channcellor,
Ja: Williames, & fra: Hawly Esq·rs· what other
Ex·ones· have ben taken by vertue of this Commis-
sion are vnknowen to vs. /

RAUFE HORSEY   JOHN WILLYAMS

FRA. HAWLEY /   [f. 188*b*

> Robte Hyde of Sherborne shomaker sworne &
> examined the XXIX·th· daye of Marche in the
> yeare afore sayde before S·r· Raulfe Horsey
> Knight & ffraunc*es* James Chauncelor sayeth as
> followeth. / vedt

That aboute Christmas Laste M·r· Scarlett, cominge to
this depon·t·s· windowe, he this depon·t· sayed, M·r· Scarlett
you have this longe p·r·ached vnto vs of the Resurrecc*i*on of
the Dead w·ch· I beleive, And if it be not soe we ar of all
men most miserable: but they sayde there is a secte that
teacheth that there is neither hell nor heaven, nor god,
nor devill; and that the soule is mortall and dyeth w·th· the
bodye. Whervnto M·r· Scarlett replied that if there should
not be such a secte the worde of god were faulce w·ch· did
teach that toward*es* the latter end there should be such
that shoulde fall awaye; but this depon·t· saieth that for his
owne p*ar*te he doth knowe noe such; neither can bringe
anye aucthoure for such reporte. but the reasons w·ch·
moved him to vuse such speches was some conference had
w·th· a brother of his, whoe dwellinge at milborne porte

toulde this depon^t that he harde Mr Davidge preache at Sturton Caundell deliu*er* in the pulpitt that there was such a sectt wch he did there seeme to confute.

To the rest of the Inter*ogatories* he can saye nothinge.

RALFE HORSEY

FFRA. JAMES. /

[f. 189

> Grace Brewer of Sherborne sworne & exami*n*ed the daye and yere last aforesaid before the sayde Sr Raulfe Horsey Knight & ffraunc*es* James Chauncelor &c.

Whoe sayeth that aboute michaelmas last cominge from Lillington in the afternone from a s*er*mon; beinge accompa*n*ied wth M^{ris} Whetcombe and one Olliver s*er*vant vnto Mr Allen of Portland castle this depon^t sayed, That they were happie that had soe good a minister. whervnto Olliver replied, that he sayed many*e* thing*es* but might have made it shorter. vnto wch M^{ris} Whetcombe aunswered if you Love to heare the worde of god you cannot be wearye wth hearinge it. Whervnto Olliu*er* aunswered I beleive in Jesus Christe and that Jesus Christ is god; but if a man beleive all that is in the scriptures he must beleive that moyses had Lii Concubines, or whores. but whether Concubines or whores this depon^t doth not well remember. but she well remembereth that she willed him to goe home & slepe for she did well p*er*ceave he was gonne wth drincke. And more to the Inter*ogatories* she cannot depose.

RALFE HORSEY.

FFRA: JAMES. / [f. 189*b*

Elizabeth Whetcombe of Sherborn sworne and
Ex*amined* before S͏ʳ Ralfe Horsey Knight, and
M͏ʳ Doctor James Chauncelo͏ʳ the XXVIII͏ᵗʰ
of M*ar*ch Año 1594.

Inp͏ʳ this deponent saith, that cominge from Lillington
about Michaelmas last from a sermon, in that afternoone,
being accompaned w͏ᵗ on Oliu*er* and M͏ʳˢ Brewer. This
M͏ʳˢ Brewer as this deponent remembreth, vsed som
speches in Comendac*i*ons of the Minister, signifieng that
they were blessed, having so good a ma*n*: wherunto the
seid Oliu*er* replied, that he vsed many word*es*, but might
have ended it in fewer, to as great effect, wherunto this
deponent replied, that he d*i*d nothing but out of the word
of god. / the word of god saith, he sayth, that moyses
had 52 whores. whores saith this deponent, nay Concubines sayd he. / whervppon M͏ʳˢ Brewer said yt was
Salomon. that he ment, and so bade him goe home to
sleepe. / And that this was all that this depon*ent* remembreth of this conference only, saving this she saith that he
said, yf he had had him in a corn*er* he could have cavyled
w͏ᵗ him. / for the rest of the p*ar*ticulers, she cannot depose,
otherwise then before she hath sayd.

R*ALPH* H*ORSEY*   E*LIZABTH* W*HETCOMB*
ffra. J*AMES*.

Theis three last are the trewe Copies of
thex*aminations* taken before Doctor James
& my selfe, the originalls remaining in the
Lo: Viscount*es* hand*es*.

R*AUFE* H*ORSEY*. /